Guidebook for Thriving in The Age of Aquarius

Companion Book to

The Ascenders

Return To Grace Series

Monty Clayton Ritchings

Copyright © 2024 by Monty C. Ritchings

Vancouver, Canada

All rights reserved.

No portion of this book may be reproduced in any form without written permission from the publisher or author, except as permitted by U.S. copyright law.

Library and Archives Canada Cataloguing in Publication

Ritchings, Monty 1951 -

The Ascenders Return to Grace Guidebook for Thriving in The Age of Aquarius

Paperback copy

Monty C. Ritchings

ISBN: 978-1-7388754-4-3

The purpose and intention behind this book

Although this book is associated with my book series, The Ascenders Return to Grace, it is not necessary that you need to have read these books.

It is my life's desire to be of assistance to as many folks as possible, to see the truth that lies before them and within them. Not my truth, but your own truth.

It is easy to feel discouraged and frustrated about the ongoing travesties expressing themselves in the world about us. They are only illusions of the lack of understanding of the Universal truths that are unfolding before us, as we move from The Age of Pisces in to The Age of Aquarius.

After all, there are only two powers in effect in the Universe. Love and Fear.

The only true path to life in the Aquarian Age is through the power of love. The love of self and the love of all else that creates this planet and the Universe. The love that empowers you to be the amazing person you were born to be. The love inside you that helps you support all others in their quest for personal empowerment through the energy of love.

No matter what belief system or religion you adhere to, the time for major change are upon you. It is up to you to choose which path you wish to follow. Again, the only choices are Love and Fear.

The concepts and tools provided in this guidebook are yours to use as you wish and to share. My wish is that you move forward in the energy of Universal Love.

An Important Notice to Our Readers

My dearest reader, I have written this book with the intention of assisting you in your own process of truly knowing yourself. By providing tools and information that I feel are pertinent to the process of revealing you to yourself, all you need is to get into the process.

I am a lay counselor and energetic healing practitioner, long schooled in the art of living. According to those that make up the rules, I am not a therapist. It does not matter to me what label is presented to identify me with others. I support all counseling practices that help individuals heal and empower themselves, whether it be in the form of established counseling, energetic healing, yoga, etc. The only thing that matters to me is that you find your own light and express it.

With this in mind, I want to make it perfectly clear that this book, any of the concepts or tools provided herein, are not meant to be a substitute for professional psychological help or any other form of intervention that may be deemed valuable or necessary in your healing journey. This statement is not meant to diminish the value of the information provided in this journal or to diminish the value of the growth discovered by my clients.

It is necessary though, to have you recognize that the lessons procured through working your journey alone are more limiting than through outside help.

I strongly urge you that as you work through the chapters and lessons in this book you obtain the support of a person capable of supporting you in your path of self-discovery.

This book is intended as a guide for you, not a replacement for the help you may need.

Remember, a candle cannot light itself. My wish for you is that your inner light be illuminated in its own special way so that it adds to the overall light of all mankind.

Monty Clayton Ritchings

Table of Contents

Section 1   The Concept of Self-realization

Chapter 1	2
Chapter 2	12
Chapter 3	17

Section 2   Our Connection with the Universe.

Chapter 1	30
Chapter 2	34
Chapter 3	40
Chapter 4	45
Chapter 5	60
Chapter 6	72
Chapter 7	84
Chapter 8	91
Chapter 9	107

Section 3   Managing Your Mind

Chapter 1	113
Chapter 2	118
Chapter 3	126
Chapter 4	131
Chapter 5	138

Chapter 6	143
Chapter 7	149
Chapter 8	156
Chapter 9	164

Section 4 Parenting

Chapter 1	175
Chapter 2	179
Chapter 3	187
Chapter 4	195
Chapter 5	208
Chapter 6	216
Chapter 7	224
Chapter 8	229
Chapter 9	235
Chapter 10	248
Chapter 11	256
Bonus- Tools For Effective Parenting	260
Summary	271

Section 1

The Concept of Self-Realization

Chapter 1

Introduction

Have you ever wondered why you were born? Or for that matter why any of us was born? And why now?

The Ascenders Return To Grace Series was written as a fun way for people to be introduced to the concept of Ascension.

The most basic premise we are working from is this:

We were born into this life (and every life) to grow and mature from the inside out.

Ascension is simply the process of elevating one's intimate knowledge of themselves more clearly, to a higher level. As one grows through the levels, their life process and purpose becomes clearer and easier; letting many of the "lies" dissolve and disappear from their life.

3

I want to assure you there is nothing religious about this process. In fact, it is almost mechanical, although it will bring you to higher levels of spirituality that you may have never experienced before this time.

We have now entered a time, actually the first time in mankind's existence on this planet, that the consciousness of mankind, generally, is in a place that supports this kind of shift, en masse.

Those of us living on the planet today are lucky enough to be the first people to live in a society that is stable enough and rich enough that we know the resources are at hand for us to survive with little or no concern. In fact, we are quite capable of thriving if we choose.

What does this mean?

In prior generations, folks had to have their mind focused at any time on survival. Jobs, keeping home, and raising kids all took complete precedent over anything else the mind could conceive. There was little time to be spent meditating about whether or not our lives were running the best possible as there was not much of a safety net to fall back on if things went sideways.

In fact, many of the concepts we will discuss in this book would never have even entered the minds of most folks back in the day. If it had nothing to do with getting through the day, it was just washed away like leftover cereal in a breakfast bowl after the meal was done.

4

Do you recall a song called "The Dawning of The Age of Aquarius"? It was released about 1967 by a music band called The Fifth Dimension. This song actually introduced the beginning of the Age of Aquarius to the world.

Fifty years later, we are eking forward in our evolution. The purpose of the Ascenders Return To Grace book series, and this companion resource guide is to assist you in speeding up your personal evolution.

Let me explain to you now, what all this means. I will break this into sections as there is a lot of information to digest.

The Dawning of The Age of Aquarius

I am asking you at this time to have an open mind to a subject that you may not have any great knowledge of, or even agree with, for whatever reason. This subject has been kicked around for as long as humans have walked this planet, and it is still here, for good reason.

No matter what your religious or non-religious beliefs are, I think we can all agree that the world and the universe are much bigger than we can perceive. Let's stretch this a little further, by suggesting that if this universe is so vast, and that, since it has not imploded on itself, there must be some form of organization that is managing it. After all, if everything in the Cosmos ran according to its own desires, we would be seeing comets and maybe even other planets bouncing off the earth on a regular basis. Or maybe, the earth could just decide on its own to make a break for it and reunite with the sun. Could be a little messy!

So, hopefully, we are in agreement with the concept that there is some kind of force that causes and maintains order in the Universe.

One of the methods we use for explaining this concept of organization is called Astrology. The basic concept of Astrology is that all astral bodies have a magnetic influence on everything else within their range. This magnetic force causes the planets to maintain the order we know.

Bringing this closer to home, if you close your eyes and sit quietly, can you tell when someone walks close to you?

Of course, you can! It is because every healthy person's body energy expands about four feet from their physical body. When someone comes close enough to enter your magnetic field, you can feel their influence.

Astrology, and in fact, astronomy, both work on the same premise. Fortunately, the astral bodies have strong enough magnetic fields that force the other bodies to maintain their distance.

Each astral body projects magnetic energy from it at a specific frequency and intensity, thereby influencing every body in its range, in its own specific manner. The influence of these bodies is constant, although sometimes the influence can vary depending on where the body is in its cycle in relation to other bodies. This is the basis of astrology.

Whew! Did you survive all that?

The next aspect of astrology to understand is that there are cycles to each of the influences. These are called houses in Astrology. These twelve houses follow a consistent pattern over and over again, ad infinitum. The twelve phases of the year, which we call months, are based on the phases of the Sun as the earth rotates around it.

Most people who do not understand astrology usually believe their "Sun" sign is all there is to this amazing and intricate process. Although very important, it is only a part.

Each of the influences of these houses impact our lives constantly. The combination of these influences at our birth, is called our birth or natal chart, the map of the solar system at the time we were born. As the rotation of the planets occur as our life continues, we are affected. However, the lay of the planets at the time of our birth has a dramatic influence on our life expression.

On a larger scale, we find Ages instead of houses. These ages are approximately two thousand years in length. I am not a Bible person, but it is convenient to use it as a good resource for explaining things and finding concurrence.

Somewhere in the Bible, in one of the passages in the Old Testament, there is a reference to Abraham killing a ram. This is very symbolic as the ram is the symbol of the sign of Aries.

The significance of this action signified the ending of the Age of Aries, which would have occurred just prior to the birth of Jesus.

Because the Ages occur in reverse to the direction of the sun signs we know, this meant that once the cusp had completed, the earth was now in the Age of Pisces.

As the Age of Aries signified the Age of Law and the development of social order, the Piscean age signified exploration and expansion through the use of the hands and the ego(mind).

We are now in the cusp of the Age of Aquarius, the age of self-realization through the combined energies of the mind and the body.

We know this is true by simply looking at how inventions have evolved over the Age of Pisces. At first, they were invented for the express purpose of improving how a person used his hands. First, the shovel was invented, now it is an excavator.

What has been the trend with inventions of the later part of the twentieth century?

The inventions focused on moving into expanding the capacity of the mind and away from hands!

The invention of the computer has allowed the capacity of the minds of humans to exponentially expand, often leaving the hands as irrelevant decorations hanging from the shoulders of the user.

As we move further into Aquarius, we will move even further away from using our hands, and even computers and such. We will not need them!

So what is significant about the time we are now living in right now?

Starting somewhere back in the 1950s, the effects of the impending transition to Aquarius began to influence our consciousness. This was demonstrated dramatically by the changes in music we listened to, the inception of the "free love or hippy" era. As well, people began protesting about such aspects of social reform such as racism and ending wars.

It has only continued and accelerated to this day, where we now think we have more than two genders of humans, our kids do not learn to write, and everybody has more rights than they know what to do with. This is all part of the expansion of human consciousness with the overall intention of getting to know oneself.

There is a darker side to this energy though. We are also seeing dramatic changes in our weather systems; critical wars are now occurring as mentioned in the Bible and the huge bureaucracies that have become the engines of our economy are vying for more control by limiting our own personal rights and freedoms.

Individual humans can often be seen exploiting others for their own benefit and to the detriment of others.

It is going to be a very interesting time during this cusp but if you can survive about two hundred more years of this escalating energy, you will get to see the outcome!

We need to go through this process in order to find ourselves. In this guide, you will find tools and concepts that will assist you in managing your life in such a way that you will have the freedom to play the game at a higher level and by initiating your own choices.

My intention is for you to see the world beyond the visible and past the chaos, into the realm of truth and self-realization.

What difference will it make?

Why do you think you are here on earth, especially right now?

Have you ever taken the time to think about your answer to this question?

9

If you have been reading the Ascenders Return To Grace series and you are now digging into this companion manual, you likely have.

This is a time of great personal questioning. Everybody is embroiled in finding the answer to this question, even if they do not realize it. Much of the turmoil we see being expressed is a result of the subconscious mind trying to find and express an answer.

Why am I here, right now?

So why should you find an answer to this question?

First, and most important to you, is that it will give you peace of mind. It will quell that feeling of restlessness you have been feeling for most of your life.

The true answer, though, lies in the concept that you were born at this time because you are a soul that chooses to advance yourself in evolution. Evolving at a soul level is our ultimate purpose in life, for as you evolve, so does the Universal Consciousness.

Why at this time?

We are in the cusp between two great ages. Cusps are times of great turmoil. Turmoil is the breeding ground for opportunities to grow. In this particular case, the opportunities are immense. The turmoil is caused by the immersion of the very different energies of each age melding into one while trying to exert their own particular brand of influence.

Some spiritual leaders claim the average person living on this planet right now has incarnated at least 1200 times previously. If this is true, then the likelihood of each of us having evolved a little is quite likely.

Being here today is like going to university for the soul.

We have all done the basics, now we can down to the heavy lifting... if we choose.

By accepting our purpose of growing, we now can have comfort in knowing there is a reason for all this havoc that is occurring in our daily lives. The purpose of this book is to assist you in understanding how to play in this life and win. Win by evolving through playing the game right.

My intention is to provide you with concepts and tools that will help you create and manifest a life that works for you and the others in your life that will help you feel joyful and satisfied, based in the energy of love.

11

What is true safety?

Chapter 2

True Safety

When I wrote my first book. Embracing The Blend way back in 2006, I realized that the first step in learning how to do anything required overcoming the inner fears manifested by the ego.

It was fascinating that as I wrote the book, I was given this little statement to include on the outer cover:

> **"We are born into safety, then trained out of it."**

Later on, I was given another section to the statement. It has become the basis of my work in self-realization. Here is the phrase in its entirety.

> **"We are born into safety, then trained out of it.**
>
> **Now it is time to return."**

In our master plan, created by the Universal forces (or whatever you want to call them), we are born safe, truly safe. It is only through the lessons of our life that we learn to no longer feel safe. People spend great portions of their wealth trying to cope with feelings and memories brought forward by events of their childhood, often with no longer-term benefit.

It is only through reprogramming the mind that we can truly move past the childhood beliefs that cause the issues wreaking havoc in our lives. In a bit, we will discuss the workings of the mind so you can begin to create the peace you desire. This peace will become one of the basic building blocks of your path to self-realization.

The Human mind is like a computer.

More accurately, a computer is actually designed to operate exactly the same way as the human mind does. The brain is our hard drive.

So what is the operating system?

Your belief systems.

That might be shocking to you, but it is the truth. Your perspective on life is primarily derived from your belief systems.

So where did these belief systems originate?

There are two arenas from which core beliefs originate in your system. The first, which we will discuss in length further along, is through family Karma. This is a much too large and important subject to cover at this point. The second, which we will focus on in this section, is through the lessons of your childhood.

Now to answer the question we left off in the last section. What is true safety?

14

True safety is what is left when your mind's software is turned off!

It is that simple! The only way to know true safety is to turn off the recordings carried in your mind's memories.

The difference between a good athlete and an Olympian is often the ability to turn off the noise in the head. This noise takes valuable energy away from the more important focus, and is very distracting.

The origins of all this software running in your head is from lessons you learned in your life before your seventh birthday.

Right from the time of your conception, you were garnering information about the rules for operating your life. At first, while in mom's tummy, you learned the rules chemically.

Since you were like an organ inside mom, everything she reacted to taught you a lesson. If mom had a good pregnancy, with lots of love, good health, and support, your chances of getting off to a good start were drastically increased. This created a healthy base for your software programming.

If the pregnancy period did not go well through activities such as trauma, poor health, poor or no relationship with the father and others, the groundwork was set for a much more challenging set of programs to work in your mind's computer.

The next event is the birthing itself. If the birthing event was positive and had little trauma, we are off to a good start.

15

The most important factor to accept in all this programming is that no one intentionally created the learning you have manifested. There is no blame. There is just life.

Most people live unconsciously. They do not realize there is any choice or any impact in any of the decisions they make, on themselves or others.

As you lived your life, particularly as a small child, the lessons were there in every moment of your life. You either created or emphasized the lessons through your reactions to the environment in which you lived.

First, it was your life with your parents, and very soon, your relationships with any siblings. Then it was on to other children, other adults, and the world around you.

As you grew and matured, you participated in new and bolder events. First, it was learning to turn over. Before you knew it, you were walking. Then it was outside with your buds, exploring this amazing world. Then it was off to school.

Every step included lessons. You were laying the foundation of your mind's software with every breath.

Some processes occurred during your maturation process as well that surely impacted your perception of life. Activities such as learning to walk, the birth of younger siblings, developing relationships with older siblings, going to school, divorce, and puberty all play a part in helping you create the expression of your life.

As you got older, the lessons were mostly reinforcements of previously learned lessons, unless it was a major event such as a serious injury, or the departure of someone close to you through death or divorce.

16

The point to this whole matter is that your mind has created this software for your life to run on, learned through every event that occurred in your early life.

Today, you will now begin to manage this software and take on the opportunity to rewrite your old programming.

You will now be able to rewrite the software in your mind so you can make a better life for yourself. You can now begin the journey of self-realization, one breath at a

Now that we have entered the energy of Aquarius, we are being invited to grow.

To grow like mankind has never grown before!

Chapter 3

Self-Realization

What is self-realization?

How is it achieved?

What is the ultimate goal?

How will you know when you have achieved self-realization?

We, as a species, have existed on this planet for many thousands of years. We lived our lives, then we died... just to be born again and go through another life. The most profound focus of our mindset was survival. We were driven to learn how to stay alive for as long as we could.

Survival is still a major influence on how we look at the activities in our lives. Depending on how we learned life as a youngster, we create and operate our life focused on survival. It is in our DNA. We are still running from sabretooth tigers!

Some people focus on amassing great wealth, while others manifest life debilitating diseases, all in the name of survival. Most of us, are somewhere in between, just trying to cope with what life appears to throw at us, trying not to get eaten by that elusive tiger.

We have lived our lives, mostly unconsciously, based on those early lessons. Many of those lessons are untrue and actually debilitating to our overall progress at any level.

Self-realization is the process of getting to know yourself, one step at a time.

Every person has a modicum of self-realization. At first, the individual becomes conscious of the basic aspects of their existence. They recognize their body is unique and separate from all other physical things. It follows them around everywhere for their whole life. They see it mature, age and decline until finally, it goes to sleep permanently.

The next step of awareness is the mind/emotions body. The person becomes aware of the activity going on inside their head. They see the outcomes of the expression of this level of consciousness, good or bad, but do not take accountability for it.

Through the combination of these levels, they live their lives. They grow up, get jobs, get married, have kids, have hobbies, travel, and all the other good stuff.

The next level is their spiritual nature. In this level, we discover our relationships with Mother Earth through nature, and interacting with other people and by questioning why we are here.

Religion was created to provide people with the opportunity to both understand and manage their spiritual aspects. People craved rules. They craved to have an acceptable understanding of their place in the big picture.

In days of old, people accepted life as it unfolded, never knowing there were deeper levels to their concept of self-realization. Life was what it was, and that was that.

Over the span of the existence of mankind, there have been many philosophers and religions that espoused information that supported a higher level of self-realization. Those who had space and desire in their lives to take advantage of these situations grew, while others just continued to survive.

Now that we have entered the cusp of The Age of Aquarius, the opportunities to grow have increased exponentially.

However, as long as people maintain the old mindset of survival, they will not understand what stands before them. They will find their lives frustrating though, because their unconscious mind is desiring to grow. Until they give this desire space in their lives, nothing will change except an increase in frustration from an unknown source.

Today, we are in a position to be open to learning new truths about ourselves. We can now become much larger expressions than ever before. We do this through the process of self-realization.

As I said before, the first level of self-realization is becoming aware of our existence, physically separate from all others. We become aware of the levels of expression we use in our lives. We believe we are those expressions.

Our concept of life is based on our body function, our looks, and how we satisfy our perceived needs to feed our bodies, mind, and emotions. This, all done without truly understanding the motives inside us that provoke our choices.

Our self-perception is tied completely to our physicality.

The next step to self-realization is in realizing that we are not our body, we are not our mind, and we are not our emotions.

So, who are we then?

For many people, these questions are too scary, so they remain stuck in the earlier form of their perceptions of life. They likely do not understand the unrest they feel inside themselves or what they can do about it, or that the restlessness is fueled by a desire to grow.

Fortunately, for all of us who have chosen to grow as individuals, there have been thousands of folks who have written books, produced workshops, and more that provide avenues for our own personal exploration. These people have set the stage for the introduction to the new life expression opportunities before us.

So what does the next stage look like?

The first step is the recognition of the feelings of restlessness they feel inside themselves. Questioning these feelings requires answers. Getting these answers requires going beyond the accepted methodologies of finding truth.

In past times, popping a pill to quell the noise was the route to take, but now, it is not enough. Actually, finding the root cause of the restlessness is required. But how?

The evolution begins.

The next first step, once we accept that we are not our bodies, our mind, or our emotions. We begin to explore the concept of who we are in truth.

Once we realize and accept the physical expressions of our lives (our bodies) are just vehicles that support us to interact in this world and we begin to treat them as such, the door opens to let us see and accept our true identity.

When we discover we are souls expressing ourselves through these vehicles, allowing us to play on this plane of existence, we now begin to walk the path to true self-realization.

So, what is the soul?

Simply put, the soul is the infinite portion of yourself. When you breathe in the first breath of life, the soul enters the body and ignites it and your life. When you take your last breath, the soul separates from this physicality allowing the body to return to the earth and the soul returns to the infinite for a rest.

The soul is the highest vibration of your individual expression. It carries the lessons you have learned from one lifetime to another, seeking an ever-expanding expression of itself.

Since everything exists as energy and all energy is part of the universe, we cannot say the soul is our piece of God within us because that is true of all energy. However, the soul, being the highest vibration of our being, is also the only aspect of ourselves with full consciousness. That consciousness is what makes the soul closest to God for it is through the evolution of our consciousness that the Universe (God) grows.

This is the purpose of our existence.

In the process of birthing, the soul enters the body to complete the connection between the Cosmos and existence on earth. The soul needs a body to connect with and to respond to life on this plane, while the body needs the soul to give it life and the ability to participate in life on this plane.

Comparably, the lamp needs electricity to make it work and the electricity needs the lamp for it to have expression.

We are here to grow, to evolve, as an expression of the Consciousness of the Universal Mind. The process we call self-realization or illumination.

Following this chapter is a basic list of steps to self-realization. It is meant as a guide to help you build your own path to knowing yourself.

In the next section, we will discuss how we are connected to the Universe.

―――――――――

Steps to self-realization

Give yourself some time to ponder each of these steps so you can gain the most from each of them as your awareness grows. You may want to return to these thoughts several times over your process.

1. Recognize and accept you feel the need for making changes in your life.
2. Be okay that it is acceptable to you that you are not perfect.

3. Connect with other people who are in their own conscious process of self-realization. As you are each ready, you can be a valuable resource to each other.

4. Connect with people who can assist and guide you in your personal growth. True growth needs a guiding light in order to stay on course until you are a master yourself.

5. Realize and accept you are not your mind, body, emotions, or any other descriptive. You are a soul experiencing a human life.

6. Learn how to be in your body consciously. What does it feel like to be in your body without actually feeling the parts of your body?

7. Learn how to manage your body, mind, and emotions so they support you in your growth and your life experiences.

8. Learn how to recognize when you are ego thinking versus conscious thinking.

9. Learn how to experience your own universal energy.

10. Create an acceptable understanding of God for yourself and how God plays in your life.

11. Take time to be quiet so you can build a conscious relationship with your energy field and your own plane of consciousness.

12. Take time to journal so you can gain clarity on whatever you choose.

13. Recognize your apparent strengths and limitations.

14. Accept that you are amazing beyond your strengths and limitations.

15. Recognize your strengths for their truth. Build on your true strengths.

16. Recognize concepts that you perceived as strengths that are not.

17. Rework your perception of your limitations so they become strengths.

18. Work to intensify and expand your personal energy field.

19. Learn to use your personal energy as a tool for expanding your abilities and your awareness of your consciousness and connection to Source.

20. Use your awareness of your personal Universal energy to connect with others so you learn to understand and accept that we are all one and connected.

21. Accept and appreciate that you are part of the universe.

Accept that you have a purpose in this life and are working to be the best you possible at any time. Life and your evolution are an ongoing process.

26

What will happen if you decide to do nothing?

What if you choose to not grow through self-realization?

This is definitely a point worth pondering since nobody is required to grow or become self-realized.

The purpose of my writing is to provide information to people who do want to change and grow with the times.

So what will happen if a person just plain says "Forget it"?

Have you ever tried to use a computer that was out of date? Got one with Windows XP maybe?

You can use the computer, maybe, if Mr. Gates has not shut the system down already. You might just find you are rewarded with a bunch of gobbledy-goop on the screen or at best, when you email the document to another computer, it may not be able to read it, or it will have to translate it into the most modern version of Windows.

Using Windows XP would be very much like writing to someone in English that only reads Cantonese. It will make no sense.

The Universe wants us to change, to become more amazing humans. In order to become more amazing, we need to deal with the issues that are presented in our lives. As we figure out how to clear these situations, we grow and are presented with some even more interesting ones. Welcome to life!

By choosing not to invest in self-realization, you still get the situations presented but you will likely not deal with them. They will internalize in your being. You will have lots of opportunities to change your mind, but if you don't, you can keep on internalizing them, until... your body or your mind cannot deal with them anymore and you get sick.

Sound tempting?

Another aspect of getting on the self-realization band wagon... or not, is the effect it will have on other people in your life.

Again, if you are working away on your computer using Windows XP and everyone else is using the most recent version, you will be out of the loop in the conversation. Nobody will speak your language. Therefore, what you have to offer will not only be of no value but could also cause harm or at least be inconvenient to the others.

One of the main methods for growth in this new age is to empower other people by providing them with positive opportunities to grow, without disempowering yourself.

We are consciously creating karma... positive karma. It is the law of cause and effect.

Staying out of the game and letting yourself just bide your time until you go to the final rest will not only not serve you, but it could create useless karma for others.

This statement is not meant to create guilt, but it is intended to get you to think about what you want out of this life you are living.

Were you just born to party and then some day die? Or were you born to grow and become something special while helping others?

It is entirely your choice.

And to finish on a positive note!

What will you gain by joining in on the Self-realization band wagon?

In one word- Clarity!

Self-realization is a lifelong process. You will not noticeably change overnight. However, you will start to find there is less tension generally in your life.

Here are some things you will gain from becoming more aware of yourself:

- As you learn to operate your body better by breathing correctly and drinking more water, you will feel better in your body, and more relaxed.

- Being more relaxed you will have more clarity of mind to make better decisions.

- You will see and interact in the relationships in your life more clearly.

- You will learn to listen to the messages your body sends you that help guide your life.

- You will become more aware of your intuitive skills and be able to apply them.

- You will adjust your life based on your inner messaging prompts rather than based on prior beliefs.

- You will be a better friend, parent, employee, boss just by being you.

- You will express the authentic version of you, powerful and safe as you manifest the best life possible for yourself.

- You will become aware of how we are all connected in the universe and use this knowledge as a guiding light.

Ponderings

Before you move on to the next chapter, please take the time to ponder over some of the aspects of the information you have just read. This will prepare you for what is coming up. You might want to keep a journal while you are working through this guide for reference at another time.

Can you relate to the feelings of restlessness in your being? If so, what thoughts keep coming up in your mind?

Do you feel the need to make serious changes to your life but are unsure what those changes need to be?

Who are you in relation to your body, your mind, your emotions?

Can you consciously feel yourself separate from these aspects?

What is the difference between true safety and protective safety? Think of some examples in your life that demonstrate both types of safety for you.

How does protective safety inhibit your ability to act in situations consciously?

How does it feel in your body when you react automatically to any situation that causes you to react in protective safety?

How does it feel when you are able to stop an automatic reaction and choose differently?

In future parts of this book, you will be provided with exercises that will assist you in increasing your ability to know and feel yourself from an energetic perspective.

Section 2

Our Connection with the Universe.

Discovering our true communications systems.

Chapter 1

Introduction

Are you familiar with the term Chakra? What do you think about chakras? Where did you learn about them?

Are chakras real? Are they just something somebody dreamed up as part of a great marketing tool for selling books?

So much of what is a natural part of the great creation we are has been unfairly relegated to the woo-woo department. Chakras are a perfect example.

Popular consensus tells us that anything invisible is only a mind toy of those who dabble in the world of fantasy. They practice meditation and do yoga... and believe that Universal love really exists.

The purpose of this section is to demystify "Chakras", a very real and important aspect of how we function and communicate on planet earth.

No matter what you personally believe is the cause of life and our existence on this planet, some things exist that we might not be able to see with the ordinary eye or accept with our finite mind.

32

The evidence that our total being is more than just our bodies and our minds is overwhelming. Even though we might try to rationalize away that which we do not understand, it still exists...now, always, and forever.

I invite you to join me on this journey into the "unknown". I ask you to walk with me with an open mind and trust that you are safe with your soon-to-be new perspective about how we really communicate, as we demystify this natural aspect of being alive and part of this great universe.

Since you are still with me after all the heavy slugging we have already worked through, this section should be pretty easy walking. Hope so!

34

There is more to life than meets the eyes.

Chapter 2

Life

Until fairly recently in western society, it has seemed to be the norm to teach children to only trust what their parents can see.

So often, young children can see "beyond the veil". However, as soon as they start talking about their imaginary friends or other occurrences their parents cannot see, they are scolded for being stupid or told that it is just their imagination and that it is not real.

Slowly and sadly, the child shuts down their innate abilities to see the larger picture of our world and joins the 'reality' of the mundane world.

Later in life when this person attempts to see the unseeable, it remains just that; for the basic concepts that were given to them at the time of their birth have been overridden with much stronger belief systems that prevent their success.

Fortunately, in recent years, the inquiring minds of adults have become more open to the concept of a world beyond that of our physical eyes. People like Lee Carroll in his writings of his Kryon Series and his introduction of the concept of Indigo Children have started to change the fear-based attitudes of people everywhere.

Children are now allowed to have their imaginary friends and even talk about formerly unspeakable occurrences.

Science is beginning to accept that the world is more than just a physical concept as well. They have even accepted that the atom, the basis of all physical life is composed of something. At least it is a start. Someday, hopefully soon, they will realize that quirks and quarks are still "made of something".

The reality is that everything that exists is composed of energy. Energy cannot be created or destroyed. It always is. It can only be transmuted or changed by a "scientific" process created by the universe.

When a log burns on a fire, it is not destroyed. It is transmuted into a simpler, more basic form of energy. That simpler form, carbon, eventually breaks down and returns to the soil and the planet it originated from. The process goes on from there, continually repeating… energy transmuting into energy of another form… but always energy.

Log on fire….. carbon… soil…. tree… log on fire… carbon… soil……

Human beings, no matter how wonderful or evolved we are, still must comply with the laws of nature. We are composed of various elements of energy. These elements manifest into specific material (or immaterial) items that are designed to perform specific tasks and form a specific portion of the total composite who is this person.

Examples are parts of your body.

Every part of our body, physical and non-physical, is created of a specific vibration of energy. Each organ is created of energy that vibrates at a specific frequency. That frequency can only produce that particular organ. Therefore, the vibration of the liver can only produce liver cells, it cannot produce an eyeball.

All objects, animate and inanimate are composed of aspects that are created by these various frequencies. The energy of these vibrations emanates from them. This is what allows medical devices to observe them.

When you pop in for an MRI, this machine observes the vibration emanated from the observed organ, not the organ itself.

Unconsciously (for most people), we feel and interpret energetic information that is projected from one body to another. Still unconsciously, (for the most part) we react to this information.

This is called communication.

38

When the mouth is open,

true communication is rarely possible.

Chapter 3

Communication

Which tells you the truth about how someone feels about you? Being told "I love you" or being kissed?

The answer is obvious, isn't it! The spoken work can be masked to hide the truth. It is also filtered by the receiver's own belief systems.... But a kiss! The truth is obvious... right through the receiver's own body.

Can you tell how someone feels about you by the way they hug you? No matter what is said, you will know the truth.

Don't get me wrong, spoken communication is an important and valid form of communication, however, to get the whole story, one must pay attention to the body language that accompanies the verbiage.

The real truth comes from reading the non-verbal communication that is being expressed during the interaction. This information cannot be altered as much as one may try. Truth will always prevail!

As was explained earlier, everything is energy. When we communicate, we speak from many different levels of vibration. These are expressed through the body. We inherently pick up information through changes in facial expression, body stance, energy projection, and hand movements during the verbal expression and after.

Now you may wonder what all this has to do with Chakras. Bear with me and you will soon see how all this is related.

Reading energetic information from the body or body language as it is commonly called is an intuitive process; however, the process of interpreting it is often perverted by the interpreter's belief systems that have developed over their lifetime through their own experiences.

To be able to access the correct information, one needs to learn to be aware of how they block or mutate proper interpretation. This requires learning to be "body aware" or "self-aware".

A large percentage of our society has unconsciously chosen to disconnect from feeling their information processing systems in their bodies. This supposedly works as a form of "protection". There have been too many hurts for these individuals, so shutting down the mind's connection to the body has become a requirement for survival.

It is all about feeling "safe."

Unfortunately, this disconnection actually does exactly the opposite of the desired effect. Being able to access and interpret the information the body communicates is vital to our survival and well-being. It is also a fundamental part of our design.

Have you ever walked past a person and instantly become afraid... even though you have never interacted with this person before?

Have you ever walked past a person and practically melted on the spot because you are so attracted to them?

These are perfect examples of how you already communicate nonverbally. Your unconscious mind picked up the information emanating from the other person, received it, and interpreted it, all without you being consciously aware.

Now that is communication! No matter how hard you try to shut down the mind-body communication system, it is there working, doing its job.

This communication system is also your "true safety" system. To truly understand the situation one is currently involved in; one must be clearly open to receiving and correctly interpreting information from all sources.

You continually communicate at an energetic level! And so does everyone else!

Your energy field connected with their energy field picked up the required information, and gave you the necessary message... all without you being consciously aware!

If you were to take the process further by interacting with these people on other levels, you would undoubtedly discover the truth about what information you received.

To communicate non-verbally (both receiving and transmitting) effectively, one needs to be aware of their own level of body awareness. The more open and aware one is, the more accurate the communication levels, as well as the effectiveness of the information.

This process is a subject unto itself, so it will be dealt with at length in the next chapter, but suffice it to say, for now, that to truly communicate, one must learn to relax through managed and conscious breathing, allowing themselves to become reintegrated and at one with themselves in their own body.

The most important message here is that, if one wishes to get a complete and accurate message, all communication systems must be open and clear of mental and emotional blockages that can potentially alter the real truth.

Understanding how the body projects information through its various levels of energetic frequency is essential to effective communication. Being body aware, relaxed and open supports the accurate interpretation of both the transmitting and receiving of information.

Now that we have a better understanding of the importance of non-verbal communication, let us move on to understanding what gets in the way of communication and how to reframe it.

43

A book that is never opened cannot be read.

There is a theme to the message in this book....

Be open!!!!

Chapter 4

Learning to be Open

We live what we believe!

If one is to be truly successful at being a good communicator, one must be open to sending and receiving messages clearly at any level.

Life does not work that way though... at least not easily. From the time we are conceived, we are bombarded with situations that require us to make decisions. Sometimes those decisions might have sounded good in the moment, but in the long run, they have may been detrimental to our own best well-being, and now limit the best expression of our life.

When these decisions are serious enough or repeated often enough, whether beneficial or not, they become core beliefs, the beliefs that form the basis of our understanding of how our life will operate.

I hope you have noticed by now that there is not one person in your life who has been able to live a perfect life. Everybody gets bent about something. That bending causes a "warp" in our perception of the world. Until we recognize the "bent" belief, it will continue to play out and skew our beliefs and our perceptions of the information we receive and transmit that form our perception of our world.

Believe it or not, even our parents are not perfect! Here is an even scarier fact... parents are human too! They are as subject to the vagaries of life just as we are... and they were once kids going through a similar learning process.

Remember back a couple of chapters we were chatting about energy transmuting where the log became carbon, then soil, and so on? Well, this happens in belief systems as well.

For example take parents 1, James and Pauline, who lived way back in the 19th century and traveled in a Conestoga wagon across the United States to find their new home.

The process was very long and arduous and continually fraught with danger and possible starvation.

From this situation, these people developed a set of beliefs that life was very dangerous, and that prosperity was not the norm, struggle and starvation were. (although the beliefs were likely already instilled previously)

It was a very long trip lasting years, as the progress was very slow. During the trip across America, James and Pauline gave birth to several children who learned about life from their parents as they continued their journey.

They learned that life was dangerous, and that prosperity was not the norm. They learned to adapt to a world where going to bed hungry and being scared was normal.

This family struggled even when they reached their final destination. Life still was not easy. They had to build a home and constantly forage for food. They had to protect themselves from the natural elements and probably other people as well.

When the children became older and married, they still carried the beliefs they had learned as children. Life was dangerous and prosperity was not the norm.

Life was far too demanding for any of these people to take the time to question their beliefs, so they continued their struggle to survive, usually living just above starving.

Generations past and now we are six generations down the family tree, somewhere around the early 1950s. Let's look at the family now.

Dad has just gotten out of the army after coming back from fighting in Korea; the economy is weak so many families are struggling to survive.

Mom has been busy trying to raise the kids while dad has been off to war. Neither parent has any social support, so they do the best they can. They have no time to become aware of their belief systems. They are just trying to survive, and not doing well with it.

They have learned well that life is dangerous, and prosperity is not the norm. It has now been thoroughly ingrained for at least seven generations.

Can you see how the energy (belief) keeps going through the same repetitious process over and over?

This belief system will continue, ad infinitum until such time as someone questions it and does what is required to change it.

The reason that it is comparable to the log...carbon...soil... tree analogy is because, the core belief has become so entrenched in the family belief system that it has become "natural" for them to believe and act accordingly, just like a law of nature.

Life is dangerous and prosperity is not the norm! The belief continues to form and express over and over because they see it occurring every day. The habit of the belief just keeps recurring again and again.

Have you ever taken the time to look at the beliefs that cause you to operate your life the way you do?

Psychologists claim that the rules we use to operate our lives are over 90% entrenched by the time we are seven years old. We learned these rules by either interacting with other people, usually our caregivers, or through direct life experiences.

We create the rules by making decisions about how we can best survive the situation we find ourselves in at the moment. Unfortunately for our older selves, these rules were decided by a child under the age of seven.

This means the rules might not be adequate for the decisions we need to make as we get older, but unless we are aware enough of this situation and how we react to it, we will continue to operate our lives in this manner over and over again, basing our life decisions on decisions learned as a child, until the day we pass on.

These rules are held in the subconscious mind. When we find ourselves in an energetically familiar situation, the ego reaches into the unconscious library and extracts the beliefs that presumably are habitually required for this current situation.

You see, one of the main purposes of your ego is to protect you. And it does a great job... according to the rules it has learned as you survived your childhood.

Now that our society has sufficiently evolved to a point where we have a safety net in case of tragedy, we are now able to take the time to question and analyze the beliefs that motivate the outcomes in our individual lives... if we choose to.

That is a roundabout way of saying that we are now at a point in society where we have the opportunity to stop and have a look at how we operate our lives, and we have the tools and support to make those changes that can make our life better. We can self-realize!

It is highly recommended that any individual who chooses to embark on a path of self–discovery find a verifiable support group, an individual counselor, and even a mentor to work with them as they dig through the depths of beliefs they have developed and integrated throughout their life.

Reframing your belief systems can be tough work and should not be entered into alone. It is a process that will likely last for the remainder of your life.

Working on making changes to your life on your own can be, at least futile, and possibly dangerous until you become skilled at managing what comes up, depending on how difficult life was for you as a child. The untrained mind cannot discern what is true or what is truly meant by the information that pops up. Be smart and get your support first.

Learning to be truly safe

The most important thing you can do for yourself, as you begin to delve into your process of re-creation is to create safety for yourself.

I truly hope you can do this in a manner that does not require medications or other limiting actions that may be counterproductive to your desire, and for your best possible personal growth and health.

Assuming you are a reasonably mentally and emotionally healthy person, safety can be created by learning to relax, learning to breathe properly, and through separating yourself from the beliefs that you are working on. I will explain these.

Learning to relax is essential. It is the first step in beginning the path of self-awareness.

To relax, it is best to create a safe place for you to do your work, where you are unlikely to be distracted by other people or other annoyances that will keep you in the "outer" state.

Make the choice to be willing to let go. Put aside any thoughts that may impede your ability to relax. Focus on the task at hand, it is the starting point for any inner work.

If the thoughts distracting you are too overwhelming, then either deal with them first, if possible, or at least write them down, so they will not feel they have been forgotten.

Sit somewhere comfortable with your back supported, hands in your lap, and feet on the floor. This is preferable to lying down as it makes it easier for you to focus and not fall asleep when you let go.

As you move into the second stage which is breathing, move your focus onto your breath, and away from the thoughts inhabiting your mind. Take deep breaths, moving your belly, for a few moments filling your body with fresh oxygen.

Make sure when you breathe you take full breaths causing the abdomen to rise. Hold the breath for a few seconds then slowly release. After a few minutes continue focusing on your breath but just breathe normally, but still belly breathing.

The third stage is one of the key points in learning to do personal growth work. Please understand and accept that

You are not your body, mind, thoughts, emotions, life, or anything else.

You just are!

I am!!!

This is very important when it comes to working with thoughts and emotions because you will not be able to let go and release or reframe the thought if you have an emotional attachment to the thought.

51

I had a friend years ago who suffered from fibromyalgia. She was consumed by this situation. Every minute of her day, the fibromyalgia was on her mind. She was consumed by trying to treat it. She went to fibromyalgia support groups. She dieted and did exercises. She did everything she could to deal with this situation... except one very important thing.

She did not let go. The fibromyalgia became part of her identity. It became part of her social network as she went to the support groups and made friends with other sufferers.

It also gave validation to her existence and gave her an excuse to not really look at the underlying issues.

Please do not do this to yourself! If you truly want to be free, you must recognize and accept that you are far more than you can possibly see or know about yourself. You are much bigger than your body, mind, emotions, thoughts, etc.

I AM!!!!

Get the help you need to manage the challenge, but do not be the challenge! It is just a temporary situation, if you let it be one!

As you sit and focus on your breath, allow yourself to relax into your chair. Continue focusing on the breath. Imagine a beautiful yellow sun above you and allow the feeling of that sun high in the sky beaming down on you. Let it fill up your entire being with its wonderful positive energy. Let it help you to relax even more. Let go! Enjoy being in your body!

When you are ready, open your eyes, take a final deep breath and carry on with your day. Smile!

It will take time to really relax. It will take time to learn to separate yourself from your thoughts and emotions. Be okay with this. It takes time to learn and accept any new belief system, especially one that challenges the old guard!

Your ego will fight this "invasive activity" as it undermines its perceived control over you.

Your ego will see relaxing as a threat because it will allow unwanted thoughts to enter your consciousness. However, eventually, when it realizes you are safe, it will settle down and work with you. You are not your thoughts, so they cannot hurt you!

It is important to note here that you do not have to delve into or analyze thoughts that come up, just recognize them, turn off the emotional connection and let them go quietly.

Learning to relax will allow you to be more open, receptive, and safe.

Once you learn to be open energetically, you will become more aware and accepting of being consciously in your body.

Another wonderful tool you can use as you do this process is to repeat the affirmation:

I know that I am safe and protected.

Repeat it in groups of threes. Do not be obsessive about it!

If you wish to be guided through visualizations that will assist you in relaxing and being more in your body, please do visit my website: www.powerfulyoupowerfulme.com.

You will also become more aware of your own energy. As you become more aware and conscious of your energy, you will be able to feel your aura and your chakras.

Now, let's get down to another unique purpose of this book.

Feeling Your Aura

To start being energetically aware, you can experience feeling your "aura" (which is an "external" part of your body energy) by doing this simple experiment:

Place your hands comfortably in front of you facing each other separated about 3 inches. Pay attention to the feeling in the space between your hands.

Next, inhale a deep breath and hold it while rubbing your hands together gently, then as you breathe out after a few seconds, separate your hands and hold them facing each other about 3 inches apart again.

Focus on the palms of your hands, then pay attention to the feeling in the space between your hands, and allow yourself to experience the feeling that has been created. It should feel like a warm magnetic feeling. That is your energy field or your aura!

A Word of Caution

Some people believe that by opening yourself up energetically, you might be opening yourself to nefarious activity from the other side of the veil.

It is essential when creating safety that safety occurs on all levels.

It is important not to poo-poo this concern. If a person has concerns about such, then, to them it is a real possibility.

We are multi-dimensional beings. We need to look after ourselves on all levels.

We are also incarnate beings (living inside a living, breathing body). That makes us king or queen of our roost.

WE HAVE ABSOLUTE DOMINION OVER OUR BEING.

No person or boogey man has more dominion than the soul inhabiting the body (that's you!). Therefore, no one or no thing can overpower another person and take over the body, or share the space or any other condition that Hollywood has trumped up… unless that person, at some level, chooses to allow it.

YOU ALWAYS HAVE DOMINION OVER YOURSELF!!

IF YOU CAN NOT ACCEPT THIS BELIEF, THEN YOU MUST WORK ON THIS FIRST.

———————

Creating Personal Safety

55

So let's chat about being safe, truly safe, not coping.

TO PROTECT ONESELF, ONE MUST FIRST BELIEVE THEY ARE TRULY SAFE.

After all, you are what you think and believe about yourself.

Secondly, one must place themselves at a highest possible level of vibration. This is done, again by breathing, visualizing and believing.

To protect yourself energetically, do this little visualization.

Breathe in deeply while visualizing gold energy flowing into the top of your head through an opening at the crown or the top of the head, filling your entire being and then emanating out of the body and filling the space all around your body for a distance of about four feet in any direction as you breathe out. Continue to do this until you feel yourself energized.

This exercise strengthens the energy field. The strongest energy field wins!

You can repeat "I am safe and protected" three times as you need as well. Good to let the mind help. This can be repeated at any time and as often as is desired.

Another thing. Good energy is always more powerful than negative energy. Boogeymen always lose!

By the way, I realize this book is not about how to visualize but I need you to understand that you do not need to be able to see in the visualization.

You just need to believe that you are doing the visualization. It is the act of doing that matters. If you can see what you are doing, so much the better.

It is important to understand that we are created safe by nature. We have been trained out of our natural safety through our experiences and choices in life.

When you become really comfortable that you are in your body, feeling your own energy and being able to increase its levels as you desire, you will be in your natural safety, as long as you continue to hold that belief in your mind.

Being protected is a different thing. It is an individual thing. Just make sure that you do not use any form of protection that separates you from your highest energy.

For example, shutting yourself off energetically from the world in a given situation is a form of protection. It does not make you safe. Safety is being connected to Divine Source through your energy exercises and by knowing in yourself that you are safe.

Emergency care workers are people who are experts at shutting themselves off energetically. They have to or they might not survive emotionally in some of the situations they find themselves in. However, when the situation is dealt with, they need to turn back on and reconnect so they can maintain a healthy connection to their life.

I think at this point, we are sufficiently ready to begin to study Chakras. Just remember, you are completely responsible for how you create and manifest in your world.

57

58

Welcome to The Ultimate and most accurate communications system!

Chapter 5

Chakras

Please have a look at the pictures on my website to get a better grasp of the subject.

www.powerfulyoupowerfulme.com

As I explained at the beginning of this section, Chakras are like hydro substations in a power grid. They collect energy from a larger source (the universe) and process the energy into a specific frequency of vibration to support communicating their individual message with the individual.

Every living being has an energy field. Animals, plants, and even the earth have an individual energy field. These energy fields are composed of various levels of energy which are differentiated by their frequency or rate of vibration.

Chakras form the various layers of the aura.

The energy which is received and transmitted through the chakra vibrates at its own unique frequency. It is a natural law that states that if two substances vibrate at the same vibratory frequency, they are the same.

In a pure, uninhibited state, the aura emanating from a living being, expresses itself in the colors of the rainbow. If you look at the picture on the website, you can see, the colors in the layers of the aura are identical and even in the same order as the colors of the rainbow.

The higher the frequency of the vibration of the color, the further it projects beyond the body.

The Politics of Chakras

Before we actually get into the explanations of each of the chakras, we have to deal with the politics. Yes, even chakras are embroiled in fighting between different belief systems.

What I present to you, I believe to be true. I believe it to be true because it is what I have experienced and what I have been taught over my 30+ years of study and practice in the field of mysticism.

You are free to choose what you want to believe though, so I will present both sides, and you can choose what you wish to believe.

First of all, some people believe that every second chakra spins in the opposite direction of the chakras on either side. I believe they all spin in the same direction. Besides having physically experienced the feel of the rotations, there is a universal rule that every field of energy, in a healthy and vital state rotates clockwise.

If a chakra is turning counterclockwise or even stalled and not turning at all, there is an issue going on that has caused that malfunction.

Secondly, some theorists claim that all of a sudden the root chakra is now horizontal instead of vertical as it has been for millions of years. My understanding is that the root chakra is the opposite end of the crown chakra, allowing energy to enter through one chakra and flow out through the other.

If the root chakra were to all of a sudden become horizontal, what would be the other end of the crown chakra?

Most important question: Why?

What would be the value of the root chakra becoming horizontal? The universe is never arbitrary, so there would need to be a valid reason for it to occur.

Have a look at the picture of the human auras on my website. This is the accepted positioning of the seven major chakras. This is how we will explain them.

The five central chakras are horizontally positioned with a back and front "door" while the root chakra and crown chakra are vertical and each other's opposite end. These two chakras are part of the system we use to "run" energy from the "sky" into the earth and back.

The Seven In-Body Major Chakras

In most philosophies and esoteric thought organizations, the number of major Chakras in the body of any living being is seven. Two major Chakras are beyond the physical body but in the auric field which also are worthy of inclusion but will be explained separately.

Generally, when chakras are explained, they are listed from lowest frequency to highest. This does not make any one Chakra more important than another. After all, we do not compare the value of information given to us by a telephone call as being more important than information we got from a book. Information is information, no matter the origin.

We all function on all energetic levels at all times as long as we are incarnate. It is only a matter of how we are functioning on each level that determines the quality and expression of information of that particular Chakra.

For now, we will focus on explaining each of the individual major Chakras. Later on, we will focus on what happens when life interferes.

The Chakras are listed below from lowest frequency to the highest frequency for no particular reason other than that is how they are usually referred to.

Please note that all of the chakras find their placement on a gland or organ that is part of the Endocrine System. This shows you the relevance of the relationship between the energetic body and the physical body.

The First Chakra- The Root

The Root Chakra is located near the tip of the tailbone but is associated with the prostate gland in men and the ovaries in women. Its color is red.

Being that the Chakra is related to the prostate and ovaries, it is easily determined that this Chakra is related to male energy and female energy in the physical form. This Chakra is related to the maleness and femaleness of the individual and their ability to ground themselves to the earth and express themselves as sentient beings (since physical energy relates to earth energy). Family energy is an extension of the energy of the first Chakra.

The Second Chakra- The Spleen or Sacral

The second Chakra is the Sacral Chakra centered in the spleen. The spleen is located on the left side of the mid-abdomen behind the large intestines. The color of this Chakra is orange.

The spleen is part of the body's immune system and works to keep metabolic balance throughout the physical being. The spleen is the Chakra of personal power at the mental/emotional level. It relates to sexuality and personal magnetism. It also relates to how a person "digests" life.

The Third Chakra-The Solar Plexus

The third Chakra is located just below the base of the breast bone. It is related to the adrenals which sit on top of the kidneys. The solar plexus actually sits above the adrenals. Its color is yellow.

The purpose of this Chakra is twofold. First of all, it expresses the energy of activation. As the adrenals activate your body, the energy of this Chakra activates your life.

The solar plexus is also the seat of Universal Consciousness and is the Chakra of highest vibration in relation to the physical plane.

The Fourth Chakra- The Heart

The Heart Chakra is located about 3 inches up the breastbone in the region of the heart. Its color is green.

This Chakra is the center of the body energetically. It is the point where the physical energy congregates with the etheric or spirit energy, the communion of spirit and body. It is the point where the energy for spiritual healing is projected.

An important note about the energy of this Chakra- It is considered the Chakra of love. The truth is all positive energy is about love so, therefore the energy for any of the Chakras is about love.

The particular energy of love emitted from this Chakra is not about romantic love. It is the energy of agape or universal love as when one gives from the heart. Any other type of love is manifested as a combination of the energy emitted by the other Chakras.

The Heart Chakra works in communion with the Solar Plexus.

The Fifth Chakra- The Thyroid Gland

The fifth Chakra is located in the center of the throat behind the hollow space in the middle. The color of this Chakra is a rich deep blue.

This chakra is located in the Thyroid Gland at the energetic point where the head energy connects with the body energy.

This Chakra is the energy of communication to the mundane or outside world as is the thyroid the communication management center for the body. The thyroid gland manages and dispenses calcium into the nervous system. The calcium is the carrier of messages throughout the total body nervous system.

The Sixth Chakra- The Third Eye

The sixth Chakra commonly called the Third Eye is located in the center of the forehead. It is actually located at this point but centrally in the brain in the Pineal Gland. The color of this gland is purple.

This Chakra is the point of the next higher level of communication namely spiritual energy or intuitive energy. It is the basis of the sixth sense.

The basic job of the pineal gland and the third eye is to provide information from beyond the physical world that is necessary to protect that person. It is how we read the energy of other beings, so we intuitively know how to interact with them and be safe.

A person can be trained to use this tool for work beyond their own being, by learning how to "see" energy and interpret it for the benefit of others.

It is interesting to note that the size of the Pineal Gland has reduced considerably in the past hundred years as people generally no longer use their "Third Eye" for processing information. This is partially caused by living in a safer environment that does not require being constantly "on guard". The other reason is that the popular consensus towards the mystical use of body energy is considered a myth since it used to be considered scientifically improbable.

The Seventh Chakra- The Crown

The crown chakra is located in the center of the brain as well, the difference being that it is a vertical chakra as opposed to the sixth chakra which is horizontal. Its color is violet.

The Crown Chakra is seated in the pituitary gland, the master gland of the physical body. Like the pituitary gland, it is the master Chakra. Its purpose is to manage all the energy of the body so that a sense of metabolic homeostasis or balance is created and maintained throughout on all energetic levels.

The Crown Chakra is the direct connection to the overall Universal Source. When a child is born it has a "soft spot" at the top of the head. This is caused due to a separation between the two halves of the skull. The purpose of this opening is to allow Cosmic information to be downloaded into the pituitary gland which in turn is transmitted to the relevant locations in the body. This information forms the basis of the life purpose and the tool kit this person will have access to while incarnate for developing and managing their own unique life.

It is also the entry point for the soul to enter the body as the first breath is taken at birth. Once the information has been downloaded, the halves of the skull grow together, usually being completed sometime before the person's seventh birthday.

It is also the exit point for the soul at last breath, for once the Crown Chakra and pituitary gland surrender to death, the soul and the physical body separate.

Other important chakras

The most important "other" chakra is the thymus gland. It is located upper mid-chest above the bronchi. The thymus gland is part of the immune system management team.

It is commonly known as the "High Heart" Chakra. It is considered the seat of the inner child, expanding its energy through laughter. Its color is royal blue.

There is some debate about which is the real heart Chakra. Again I reiterate, it is up to you. I feel they are kindred spirits of the same energy but serve slightly different purposes.

The heart Chakra is more centered and therefore more grounded for healing purposes. The high heart is higher so more connected to spirit energy and healing on a spiritual level.

In healing there are also minor Chakras located in the elbows and knees that can be used to assist in managing the movement of energy along the limb.

The last minor Chakras are in the bottom of the feet. Their purpose is to work as a gateway allowing the energy from the body to flow into the earth and vice versa. They are an important tool in our process of being grounded to the earth.

The two sides of the Chakras

Each of the Chakras has two ends to it so that energy can flow in and flow out as needed. It is my understanding that the energy flowing through the horizontal chakras (2-6) enters the body through the opening in the back and is transmitted through the front.

To me, this makes sense because the bulk of our communication is performed from the front of the body; however, we certainly do have access to information from the back, especially if someone is sneaking up on us.

As we have said before, the Crown Chakra and the Root Chakra are opposites of each other. However, energy flows in either direction through the Chakras as sky energy flows into the body down through the Crown Chakra while the body receives and absorbs earth energy through the Root Chakra via the legs and feet rising back up the body through the spine, up through the head and back out.

The Nine Chakra System

The seven Chakra system only deals with the energies of the Chakras in the physical body as we have discussed above.

In recent years, many metaphysical and mystical philosophies have realized that in teaching about the Chakras, there is an important need for us to realize and work holistically. We must therefore include the auric field as part of the sentient being's package.

A healthy human's aura expands about four feet beyond the visible body in any direction. (That is why you can feel other people when they move closer to you.)

It is now recognized that two other Chakras are also major Chakras but resident only in the auric field. They are:

The Star Chakra

. It is found about 18 inches directly above the Crown Chakra. It is the unique connection for the person between themselves and the universe. This energy, because it comes from the sky, is considered positive in polarity.

The energy from the universe flows into the Star Chakra, then flows down into the Crown Chakra and into the body. It is the only major Chakra found in the person's energy field above the head.

The Earth Chakra.

It is found at the other end of the auric field, 18 inches below the earth. The purpose of this Chakra is to help the person ground themselves to the planet, just like roots to a plant. The polarity of the energy of this chakra is negative in polarity.

One can make a comparison to explain the value of the Star Chakra and the Earth Chakra by comparing our body to an apple. The end of the apple that is connected to the tree is of negative polarity as it is pulling energy from the earth through the body of the tree. The fly end of the apple is the positive end as it draws energy from the air.

There may be other Chakras that are alive and functioning in our energetic field, however, for the purposes of this discussion, those mentioned above are the most important.

Now that we have completed our discussion on Chakras themselves, we can move on to how Chakras function in our lives.

Relationships are about sharing energy.

Chapter 6

Relationships- from an energetic perspective

Earlier in this book we discussed how everything is composed of energy. We also learned that how we discern one thing from another is by translating the information we receive from its unique frequency into understandable messages that we interpret as we require.

If we were capable of seeing the world, and in fact the universe, as energetic vibrations, we would see multitudes of streams of energy flowing from one object to another.

Everything that exists communicates by this means. However, we are only able to interpret information that is within a specific vibratory range. Can you imagine how overwhelmed our brains would be if we could receive and interpret all vibrations?

Our chakras receive and transmit the energy of specific frequencies. These frequencies are contained within the range of frequencies that we can interpret.

The purpose of this chapter is to discuss how relationships function from an energetic perspective.

When we interact with another person, our chakras automatically check them out. When the energies connect, information is transmitted and received by both people instantly. This information is interpreted by each person according to their personal belief systems, to instantly determine what kind of relationship might be available with this other person.

Have you ever entered a room full of people and been automatically attracted to one specific person? What did you feel? Where did you feel it in your body?

Have you ever run into a person and immediately felt negative energy from them, maybe so bad that you turned and removed yourself from the situation?

How do you feel when you encounter someone you know really well?

These are examples of the energies emanating from your chakras picking up information from the other person's projected energy. The information is then interpreted according to your engrained belief systems.

We only connect on specific levels of energy with each person we have a relationship with. Depending on the depth and dynamics of the relationship, this energetic bond can be very minimal or extremely deep.

Each relationship has an individual set of connections as well. This connection can change, but the first connection usually has the most impact on the long-term definition of the relationship.

The more chakras that connect, the bigger the connection and, depending on the level of personal and spiritual development of the individuals, the more significant and conscious the relationship can be.

All people connect energetically in this manner; however, it depends largely on the "maturity" of the individuals to be able to recognize the chakras they connect on and how they will manage the flow of energy between them.

After all, just because the two people connect on certain levels does not mean the relationship is relegated only to that certain connection. Exploration by both parties regarding the feelings they perceive can redefine the parameters.

People who are not open or are not very developed spiritually will not connect very well with others in the upper chakras. They will connect mostly on the lower three physical chakras.

People who are not very well connected to the earth will not connect well with the energy of others through the lower chakras but might with the upper chakras. These people would be considered "not grounded", at least not in this particular relationship.

Depending on how the chakras operate in each individual, the connections will vary as to how they are connected. It can also be influenced by how each individual is feeling at the time.

Two people who connect really well only on the highest chakras will have a great relationship doing altruistic activities or studying different subjects or enjoying meaningful conversations. They will not likely have any substantial kind of physical relationship.

Two people who connect very well at the lower chakras might have a very physical relationship with a lot of mental and emotional activities, but they will not discuss great philosophical subjects or do spiritual healing together.

All of this is ok. Every relationship is unique and subject to change. We need to accept this fact and be ok that we cannot have meaningful conversations with some people, and we cannot have sex with everybody. It just makes life much more interesting.

An interesting and important note to appreciate is that we do not connect deeply with all people. We inherently have the automatic capacity to withhold our Chakra energy and only transmit it when a connection of value occurs.

Two people passing each other on the street might just skim their auras past each other, and nothing more. They might pick up some quick information but likely nothing very substantial.

This is so important because if we were to allow ourselves to connect with everyone, we would become very tired quickly from all the exertion. It would also be very hard to focus on tasks, as we would not be able to focus on what we were trying to do. We would be so busy processing all the information that we could not focus on our real tasks.

Chakra energy and core beliefs

As was mentioned in an earlier chapter, what our memories hold affects how our chakras operate.

We all have had traumatic lessons in our childhood. These lessons have caused us to make very serious decisions that may impact our perspective of life until the day we pass on.

In a perfectly spiritual person, all of their Chakras are open at the right level, turn in the right direction at the appropriate speed, and receive and transmit information appropriately.... There are very few people on our planet like this today.

The rest of us live our lives having our Chakras opening and closing as we process our stuff. However, sometimes "our stuff" is too much; causing our mind and the related Chakra to make the choice to shut down or even cause the Chakra to revolve backward on a long-term basis.

This situation is or should be of great concern to people who suffer from this choice... and it is a choice!

By nature, our Chakras are open and happily turning continuously in a clockwise manner. People who have suffered events in their lives such as sexual and physical abuse or abandonment will find themselves struggling to allow their lower Chakras to be open.

People who struggle with feeling safe due to events that caused them to experience neglect or rejection will often struggle with issues related to their higher chakras. They will only believe in things they can see.

When Chakras are closed for extended periods, serious issues can develop in the person. The parts of the body related to the Chakra can become either seriously depleted or overloaded with energy that is not being allowed to process as designed. A prolonged lack of energetic balance cannot be sustained as the body will fight to regain metabolic balance through the actions of the Endocrine System.

Many of the conditions we suffer from over our lives are related to the improper flow of energy through the Chakras. After all, everything that exists is energy in its own unique form and it always strives to maintain that form. When the chakra is closed or reversed, the energy is also held internally or spins in reverse. Long-term activity of this sort can lead to severe health issues.

This fact is a key to understanding our health. The more open our chakras are overall, the healthier we will express as an individual. Developing and maintaining a healthy mindset is an absolute must for good health… and it is rarely too late to start, even if your health is already being challenged.

Relationship Issues

Until I get around to writing it, there is no book that explains the rules of life.

Unfortunately for the world, it is not on my list of writing aspirations, so everyone will just have to keep limping along trying to figure it out for themselves. Maybe this book you are now reading will become a close shot at it!

I wrote a book several years ago called **Embracing The Blend**. Its focus is on Core Beliefs and how we learn relationships.

As I have said before, we learn the bulk of our core beliefs that form the structure of our belief systems and our life interpretation system before our seventh birthday.

One of the major lessons we learn, and it is a very slow lesson with many layers, is about how relationships work. We learn the rules mostly by watching our parents and somewhat less from other adults and our siblings that play in our lives.

We learn to be primarily one of four relationship characters:

- Like dad
- Like mom
- The opposite of dad
- The opposite of mom

If you watch yourself or any other person you know really well, look at how they do their relationships. See if you can pick out which character they have chosen to emulate.

For people like me, having had four parents as I grew up, it is a little difficult to pick out, but I definitely can see aspects of each of my parents as I evolve.

Having come to terms with my life now, though, I do recognize I have a similar life expression to my father. Fortunately for me, I have chosen to express my life in an inclusive positive manner, unlike my father who lived only to satisfy his own needs.

This is not cut and dried. You will also pick up characteristics from other significant teachers, but there is always a primary character. For instance, one of my high school teachers wrote her capital "F" backward. I thought that was neat, so I copied her… to this day!

Now here is the part that makes this learning process really suck!

Mom and dad were not perfect! They had no better idea what they were doing than their parents did! They did the best they could. Now the job is yours to figure it out!

In most childhoods, the person will be attracted to their opposite parent. Boys, especially, are really taught to be needy of their mother's attention while girls learn to rip their father's hearts out with their beautiful little eyes that entwine right around their father's brains.

So boys learn to grow up needing mommy's approval and girls learn to manipulate men by being cutesy. Then life intervenes!

Boys don't get enough of mommy's approval and daddy and other brothers compete for the limited amount of approval mommy has to dole out.

Girls find daddy working long hours to keep the family fed so they feel neglected and unloved. When mommy tries to horn in on their territory, the rivalry starts.

This is exaggerated, but it is the world of relationships. As each child winds their way through their childhood, they learn how to build relationships by watching mommy and daddy and by doing whatever they feel they need to do to get their needs met.

All these lessons are contained in the subconscious mind. These lessons manage how each individual responds to their world around them. Their Chakras react to these beliefs.

Children who have to compete for a parent's attention and approval continuously will develop extra-wide Chakra openings, so they can grab whatever energy they can get.

Children who are neglected, abused, and otherwise mistreated may choose to close a particular Chakra in an attempt to preserve the energy.

It is all about safety!

This is why it is so important for children to be raised in an environment with two healthy loving parents who have the time, capacity, and willingness to consciously raise the child to be healthy on any level as a person. It is the only way a child can grow up to be a fully functional adult without having to do a mess of emotional and mental reframing work.

We discuss this matter in a later section of this book focused on raising healthy children through conscious parenting.

When people interact with each other, they unconsciously attempt to link up the corresponding Chakra energy. Each person's energy "feels" the other person's energy system for commonality in need.

A girl might need a father figure so is attracted to a boy who is really demonstrative of his manliness. The relationship is great… until the humans enter!

She finds out his manly façade is an illusion while he finds out she is not willing to give him enough mother energy.

Each individual struggles to have their needs met unconsciously. This causes an energy rivalry that boils over into the real world. Neither knows how to manage the situation to have their needs met, and neither of them is capable of understanding what their partner's needs are.

As this is going on, the energy of the Chakras is going crazy trying to find satisfaction and fulfillment.

Finally, the relationship is a bust. She is off to somewhere else, and so is he. Does it just end, and everyone carries on? Not likely.

Each of them has mentally and perhaps physically chosen to leave the relationship, but did they disconnect at the Chakra level?

The likelihood is no they have not. Here are some likely outcomes:

- One will feel great emotional and possibly physical distress since the Chakra is not being fed as it desires. This can really physically hurt!

- One will run off into another relationship thus disconnecting from the first partner and immediately connecting with a new source of the required energy leaving the energy cords of the Chakras of the other flailing in the wind.
- One could feel very angry having their energy source revoked and do all kinds of stupid things that they will live to regret... like posting unkind things on Facebook or worse!

There may be more possible outcomes, but these will give you the idea.

The problem with this situation is the people involved in the relationship do not understand how we interact on an energetic level. They do not understand how we draw energy from others to satisfy our own needs and then feel like we are falling apart when the energy source disappears.

So what to do?

If people understood how we interact energetically and how the energies of each person intertwined with each other, they could learn how to choose and manage relationships, and more importantly learn how to manage their own energetic needs properly.

This conversation points to a very important aspect of relationships. Maturity! Just because a person has hormones firing in overload, does not mean they are mature enough to hold the energy in a serious and intimate relationship. There must be a balance between the maturity of the person in mind and emotions along with the physical in order to have the capability of coping and managing a relationship in a long-term and healthy manner.

Would it not be better for young adults to enjoy being young and free instead of trying to cope with life by acting like the adults they are yet to become?

I think at this point we will leave this subject to a chapter of its own. So let's take a deep breath, forgive ourselves for not knowing all this stuff before we jumped into relationships, and get ready to create a new way of living.

84

Meeting The Full You

Chapter 7

Working With Your Own Energy

Much of the information in this section is directly related to the earlier chapter on self-realization. It is still a worthwhile read because it is discussed from a different perspective.

All through this section, we have repeatedly been talking about universal energy and how everything is composed of this wonderful aspect of the Divine.

Like everything that exists, we use energy, and we need to recharge ourselves. We need to breathe properly. We need to eat. We need to drink water. We need to sleep, and we need to live our lives. All these things renew our energies on various levels. However, they cannot recharge the energy we need and use the most... our divine energy.

For what reason, I do not know but somewhere in the past, we seem to have forgotten that we are part of the Divine Essence. We are designed to recharge our divine self directly from Divine Source.

86

Somewhere along the way, it became common to attempt to access our Divine energy through our interactions with other people or by having lovable pets to scratch their backs or rub their bellies. This process works as long as everything is perfect, but what a mess when things go sideways.

Just like in the example in the previous chapter, attempting to source this high level of energy from other people can come at a very great cost. So the question is "How do we do it without all the drama?"

It sounds simple, but the answer takes work. We need to reconnect with the Divine Source, with the Universal energy that is innate in our being and the universe as a whole. We need to learn to hold our connection with the universe so that we are constantly and consistently replenished at this very important level.

There are many aspects to this process. We will go through each one, so you can understand what needs to be done to feed yourself.

First of all, I feel that I must state emphatically that this process does not require a belief in any religious organization. These organizations are man-made and do not generally provide the necessary connection for this process.

It is possible, however, for a person who is truly devout in their religion to become inspired to allow divine connection through the lessons they have been exposed to in the process. This occurrence will enhance their relationship with their God.

It is important though, to realize and accept that there is a greater consciousness than our own. I will refer to this as Divine Intelligence or Cosmic Consciousness or maybe even God, however, please just accept that I am referring to the same point of source.

I will not attempt to define these terms since they are extremely personal in nature. It is my desire for you to develop your own definition and therefore your own relationship with the "God of Your Heart".

Secondly, it is important to realize and accept that we are innately a part of this Source. We cannot opt out. We might choose to close our minds to this truth and not benefit from this extremely important aspect of ourselves, but it is there no matter what, and you have a relationship with it, no matter what.

Every level of energy that composes who we are is Divine Energy. By accepting this fact, we automatically open ourselves to the connection we have with Source.

The next step is to understand that we can manage our relationship with these various energies. In fact, we already do this through our thoughts and belief systems. The task is now to work with these energies consciously.

As we have spoken about in previous chapters, our mind can open, and close chakras instantly as suited by any particular belief we hold.

In that, we must be vigilant about our thoughts. We need to question everything we believe until we have reframed any thought that exists in our mind that separates us from our true selves and Divine Source.

This process may be scary. The ego (which has become highly overworked in our society) will resist change, but by carefully, consistently, and lovingly learning and applying tools to change your beliefs and your habits, you will consciously reconnect with the flow and expand your relationship.

88

Working with a person who is well trained in helping you reframe yourself is absolutely essential. Programs like Core Belief Engineering are wonderful and safe tools for making the changes you desire as is The Body Code.

Why do you want to do all this work?

Firstly, so you will feel absolutely great about your life no matter how it is flowing. Changes in how you do your life will be easier because you are more aware of what needs to change as you choose to evolve yourself. Having a good toolkit really helps!

Secondly, because it is what you are here to do.

Thirdly, this is how Divine Consciousness grows. As you grow, it grows because it experiences through you… and everyone else.

Once you can get past your ego and your fears of change, you will find that everything in your life will improve. You can use the feeling of fear as a tool rather than a limitation.

The true purpose of the feeling of fear is one method the subconscious mind has for telling you that you do not have enough information about the matter you are focused on.

For example. Back in my truck driving days, I stopped by a gas station for fuel. When I came into the station, the young lady working at cash, looked at me aghast. She asked me if I really drove that big truck. She then went on to say she would be far too afraid to drive such a big machine.

A couple of weeks later, I happened to be back in the area, so I dropped in to see her. She was quite flabbergasted as she recognized me, and that I was driving a considerably bigger truck.

I asked her if she recalled the conversation we had had previously. She nodded and then I asked her if she understood what fear means when it is expressed. I told her the statement above, then asked her what she could do if driving a big truck was important to her.

She thought about it for a minute, then said she would go to a driving school. I laughed and congratulated her! I told her that is the process of dealing with fear in any situation.

Get the right information and the fear goes away!

Relationships will change too because once you learn to source your energy from the Divine Source, you will no longer be dependent on other people for your continual fix.

You can let go of the fear of not having enough!

You will also choose healthier relationships with other folks who are consciously connecting to Source. You will not find them as wearing, so you will enjoy being with them more.

This does not mean that you will not want to have relationships; it only means that you will not **need** relationships any more than you need any other addiction. Your relationships will be by choice, not by need.

Relationships will become lighter, more fun, more meaningful, support more personal freedom, and will last longer. Does that make it worthwhile? And you can choose to do many of those things you feel are important to you without feeling guilty.

While we are working on the emotional/mental aspects of reconnecting with Source, there are exercises one can do to facilitate the process. These are included in the next chapter.

I sincerely hope you are having fun with this bundle of information I have put together for you. I am sure you have a lot of food for thought!

91

The higher the vibration you absorb and emanate, the safer you are. The reason for this is that one cannot hold victim energy, which is a low energy form in a high state of Universal or Divine Energy, as they are incompatible.

Chapter 8

Exercises for Working with Source

Now we get down to the fun!

The most important thing for you to accept during this process is that you are now doing what you naturally do anyway, only your ego-based training is being set aside. These exercises are perfectly safe.

An important note to realize and accept when working with Divine energy is that you are raising your own energy to a higher level than you have consciously known before.

The first aspect we are going to look at is the physical. Working in the esoteric realm requires cooperation from the physical body and the physical environment to be able to relax and allow yourself to let go.

You may have experienced yoga and/or some types of meditation. One of the first things they will say to you is that position is everything. I am going to explain why this is true.

As has been stated before, energy flows up and down the body through the nervous system. Sky energy flows in from the Star Chakra into the Crown Chakra and down the body into the earth and the Earth Chakra and vice versa so it returns to the Star Chakra.

For the energy to flow properly, the body must be positioned properly. This is not just true for allowing the energy to flow, it is imperative all the time. Correct posture is vital for proper body performance.

When the posture is correct, there is less resistance between the body parts and the internal flow of energy. It also allows you to focus on the job at hand more easily because there will not likely be any body parts screaming because they are uncomfortable.

The most important concern is holding your head over your shoulders so that your shoulders and neck are straight, not slumped or pushed forward. The reason physically for this is because correct posture takes the pressure off the muscles in the neck and shoulders as they try to support the weight of the head. Energetically, the point in your neck where the Cervical Vertebrae connect to the Thoracic Vertebrae at the base of the neck is a point where the energy traveling up and down the spine can become blocked if this point is not open.

Have you ever heard of someone being called a "head case"? This is caused by the flow of energy being cut off either at this point or if the Crown Chakra is closed or both. The energy becomes trapped in the head as it is unable to flow into the body.

The second aspect of physical form that is important is having the spine relatively straight. Now. this is not meant to be a form of punishment and it is not meant to be uncomfortable. It is necessary to keep the flow of energy moving up and down the body as easily as possible. Again, poor form can cause restrictions in energy flow and may draw your attention away from what you are attempting to do.

Be lazy! Do it right! It takes far less energy to do it right than to do the habitual form that causes you stress and discomfort.

Each of the Chakras is located in a specific organ or gland that is related to a specific vertebra in the spine. Incorrect posture will limit the flow of energy and causes unnecessary discomfort.

When doing energy work it is always preferable to be in a vertical or semi-vertical position such as sitting. If you have difficulty holding your back reasonably straight when you are sitting, place a cushion behind your back or find somewhere different to sit. You should also be able to place your feet squarely on the floor with your hands separated in your lap.

Lying flat during any kind of meditation or mental visualization process is acceptable but not recommended because it is too easy to fall asleep and **harder to remain focused.**

Next important aspect in the physical.

Making sure that your body is fueled properly is essential for all aspects of living. Connecting with Source requires it too!

Water. Being hydrated properly is essential. After all, we are primarily composed of water. The energy we are working with travels better in a hydrated body, besides, it is easier to concentrate if you do not have a dry mouth.

Most important- Breathing. For some reason, we as humans have forgotten how to breathe properly. We have become lazy in our breaths and are paying the price for it.

Most people seem to breathe using only the upper portion of their lungs. You can check yourself just by focusing on how you breathe mechanically. What is moving when you breathe?

If only your lungs and chest are moving, then you are not breathing properly.

Breathing must include moving the muscles of your abdomen. By raising your abdomen as you breathe, it forces the toxins and stale air in the bottom of your lungs to be expelled.

If you take nothing else from this book, learning to breathe properly is the one thing you must learn.

Breathing completely is not just to be done while you do these exercises. It must be done all the time, every breath you take. You will be amazed at how much better you feel!

Next Step

Visualizing

Now let's get down to the purpose of this chapter. It is time to learn how you can actually work with your own connection to Divine Source. First of all, though, we need to have a common understanding of the words we are using so that the message I am providing makes the best sense to you.

Definitions

Before we begin to work with visualizations I am going to clear up some misconceptions. There are two of concern at the moment.

First of all: Meditation, Contemplation, and Visualization

They are not all the same. These are my definitions.

Meditation is a relatively passive process whereby the "meditator" quiets themselves down and brings themselves into a quiet, relaxed state by continually repeating a chosen chant or mantra. This person may stop chanting and just remain quiet after the chanting and enjoy being connected to the universe until they choose to return to the mundane or outer world.

Contemplation is a similar process to meditation except it is slightly more active. In contemplation, the "contemplator" chooses a particular subject they want to connect with and focus on during this process. They could contemplate any subject they choose from "love" to "solving a mystery" in the process of contemplating. The purpose of contemplating is to discover some new knowledge related to the chosen subject.

Visualizations are the most active process of the three. They are often called "Guided Meditations, however; they are not true meditations as there is an active component to them. There are many, many types of visualizations such as the ones you are about to learn below.

Visualizations are often tools used for performing esoteric projects. This could include healing facilitation, psychometry, projecting energy, astral projection, and many others. They all act as a vehicle for connecting with and using Divine Source.

Visualizations that are called Guided Meditations are often used as relaxation techniques or training techniques to help people learn to visualize.

Now, the second definition I am sharing with you is "visualization". This word is an absolute misnomer. According to the word, it means that you need to be able to visualize or "see" what you are working on.

What if you are not a visual person? Does this mean you cannot do visualizations?

The term "visualization" actually refers to sensing your way through the process, sensing by whichever tool(s) or senses you choose to use.

You could use any of your senses singly or combined in the process of visualizing. These would include seeing, hearing, feeling the non-physical, feeling the physical, tasting, and smelling. As you become more comfortable with working with various visualization processes, you will learn which senses you are most attuned to. None is any better than the other. It is just about getting the job done!

Rules for using Visualizations.

One other really important aspect about visualizing.

You must let go!

Visualizing is much like mailing a letter. First, you recognize the thought that is to become the letter, you write the letter and put it into an envelope, **then you put it in the mailbox and…. You let it go!**

If you miss any one of these steps, you did not complete the task. The Universe cannot help you if you are attached to your message.

Next and just as important… the message must be in present tense. If you send a message to the universe written in future tense, the reply will be… (big universal yawn) "Okay, whenever you are ready, let me know".

When you are doing visualizations, intention is always essential.

Visualizations require a clear mind and heart.

Visualizations only work if the intention is for the absolute good of whom it is intended for and why it is being projected.

If you just robbed a bank, doing visualizations will not clear your energy field. This process is not a way of escaping self-responsibility.

However, if you or a friend is not feeling well, sending them some energy to help them move their energy to a higher level will work.

It is always best to send energy to others with no expectations. Just like mailing the letter, if you expect something back, you did not let go. Also, if your intention is not honorable, it will not work and may even backfire causing you repercussions.

Be clear. Be honorable. Let go.

Now, here are some visualizations for your use. Learn the process so you do not have to read it. Your process does not have to be exactly as I have laid it out. The objective is just to get you doing it.

100

Visualizations, even if you do not see them are hosted on what is called the "Screen of the mind".

When you are doing the process, pretend there is a movie screen inside your forehead.

This is the place where all the activity starts and flows from. Remember to keep yourself separate from the visualization. It is an action. It is not you. The pictures, thoughts, and emotions are just tools for getting the job done. Remember to keep them that way!

Practical Visualizations

Safety Visualizations

Believing that you are safe on any level is absolutely essential to living life fully and especially when you are working on the esoteric planes. Believing you are truly safe allows you to relax and be more engaged in your process.

This visualization is an example of how you can raise your energy to help you feel safe. Please note that it is always up to you to believe that you are safe and to do something about it if you do not feel safe.

Your belief about your safety is the basis of your ability to actually be safe.

While you are learning how to do this visualization, please sit down somewhere quiet where you feel safe and comfortable. Once you are more comfortable with the process, you can do it anywhere and anytime you choose. You won't even need to close your eyes. You just do it.

This process can take as long as you choose to take and can be done as often as you feel necessary.

Here goes!

Safety Cloud

Sit quietly somewhere comfortably. Take a few moments to relax by focusing on your breath. As you relax, visualize yourself immersed in a golden cloud that completely envelopes you, inside and out. As you breathe, continue to feed more golden light into the cloud knowing that you are accessing this energy from the Universal Source.

When you feel that your energy has been brought up to an acceptable level, just take a deep breath, exhale, open your eyes and carry on with your day.

You can repeat this mantra if you choose as well:

"I know that I am safe and protected".

It should be repeated in groups of three times and may be repeated as many times and as often as you wish. Be mindful not to be obsessive about it though, as that undermines the objective.

Safety Ring

Same procedure as the Safety Cloud, only visualize a physical ring circling yourself about 4 feet from your body.

The difference in use between the two visualizations is that the Golden Cloud (preferred) provides the energy for general non-specific safety as its purpose is to raise your energy. The Golden Ring is used in specific cases when you are putting yourself into a situation of potential danger.

The Golden Ring should only be used in specific situations (of your choice) because it actually limits the flow of Universal Energy in both directions. This limits your ability to send and receive information and is managed by your ego as it is a physical protection device.

This process should only be used short term while you physically remove yourself from the situation. It should be used in conjunction with other safety techniques, such as feet moving away from the situation as soon as possible.

Once an acceptable distance has been completed, do the Safety Cloud to raise your energy and get out of fear mode.

Mind and Energy Management Visualizations

If you go to my website https://powerfulyoupowerfulme.com/videos/ you will find some easy-to-learn tools for working with Chakras. Please enjoy them and use them as often as you can. The purpose of these videos is so you can learn these tools so you can use them any time you want. Share them with others, especially your children!

As a point of reference, to me, an open Chakra feels magnetic, just like how you felt when you did the exercise feeling the energy between your hands.

A closed Chakra produces no energy while a reversing Chakra feels uncomfortable.

Opening Your Crown Chakra

The first tool is reconnecting with the Universe when you feel you have become a "head case". You will know if you are currently in this mode because you have thoughts that seem to absorb your attention. You might feel disconnected with the world around you.

To relieve this situation, it is necessary to re-open the Crown Chakra. I will describe it here; however, I truly recommend seeing the video on my website.

Touch the pads of your right thumb and right first finger together. Pretend you have a piece of yarn in between your fingers. Raise your right hand about 6" over your head.

Form a circle repeatedly in this position about 4" in diameter in a clockwise direction. Slowly wins the race. Repeat this as long as you wish, and then lift the end of the yarn up to connect with the Star Chakra which is 18" above your head.

Once this is completed, take a deep breath and let go. You just became a trolley bus running on Universal Energy.

Remain sitting quietly for a minute and allow yourself to feel the introduction of the energy into your body. Try to feel your mind quieting and your body relaxing.

Managing Your other Chakras.

It is essential for your best health and connection with the Universe that all of your Chakras be open properly and functioning fully. As you learn to experience your own body energy you will be able to intuitively determine whether each of the Chakras is open or not.

To open any of the Chakras, just position your hand in the same manner as mentioned above in front of the chosen Chakra. Rotate your hand clockwise slowly for a few seconds. See if you can feel a difference.

For the rear of the Chakra, you will have to do the same exercise except visualize it.

For the Root Chakra, remember to point downward.

If you find that you seem to be unable to feel the Chakra being open, you might consider doing some journaling or other type of introspective activity that might help you understand what belief is active that relates to the Chakra. A good growth opportunity!

Opening the Earth Chakra

Much as opening the Crown Chakra by reattaching to the Star Chakra allows you to access sky energy, you can do the same process with the Earth Chakra.

By intentionally connecting with and opening the Earth Chakra, you can help yourself to be more grounded to the earth.

Place your right hand in front of you with your fingers pointing down. Position the pads of your right thumb and first finger together. Move your hand in slow clockwise circles for as long as you choose while mentally connecting with the Earth Chakra.

When you are ready raise your hand as if you are pulling up the earth energy. Feel it rise into your feet, legs, body, neck, head, and beyond to the Star Chakra.

A variation to this action is to use the Chi Gong movement for grounding. This is completed by stretching your arms out to your sides. As you breathe in, you push your arms down to the earth with your palms facing down.

108

As you breathe out, turn your palms over and draw your arms back up like swooping water over your head.

Release and enjoy the moment of quiet.

Once you understand and accept the reality and purpose of the Chakras, you will never look at life the same again.

It will be much better and more fulfilling!

Chapter 9

Summing it up

Now You can Watch The Earth Turn!

We all have a choice at any time about how we live our lives and how we perceive our relationship with everything that exists. We can choose to live our lives completely based in the mind and the physical realm and live what we believe is a "full" life.

We can also choose to see and participate in life in the greater picture by acknowledging and accepting that the world we participate in is much larger than we can perceive through our physical senses.

By accepting the much larger picture of life, we allow ourselves to be much larger than previously. We also allow ourselves to live healthier lives on any level. We also get to include other previously unattainable activities in our lives because we are open to a new and higher source of inspiration.

You never know what will come to you as you open yourself to these new layers of life. More connection with others, more connection with Mother Earth, and more creative activity in your life will all be yours as the lotus flower blossoms inside you.

Will you find your life problem free? Nope. You now have more tools to understand what lessons have become apparent in your life, so you can see it for what it really is rather than the old limitation that it used to appear as.

You now have the opportunity and the skills to embrace life as a joyful event whether you are struggling with a growth opportunity or taking the time to smell a flower.

My hope for you is that by providing the information in this section for your learning pleasure you will broaden your relationships with all that exists so that you can come to enjoy the real world of Universal Energy, and of course that you will come to know and embrace the real you.

As you work through the remainder of this book, try to remain aware of the non-physical body and any energetic reactions as they express.

We will now move on to the next section where we will explore more about mind management, focused on keeping yourself in your body by using specific tools for managing stress.

Before we do though, let's see if you got the gist of this section. Time to ponder again!

113

Ponderings about Chakras and Body Energy

Are you aware of your body energy?

If you rub your hands together, can you feel the magnetism between?

When doing visualizations focused on your body energy, can you feel the difference when you expand your body energy?

Do you find it easier to be conscious of being in your body?

Do you find it possible to feel your energy field?

How do you define Chakras?

Can you feel them in your body?

Have a look at a Chakra Chart alongside of an Endocrine Chart so you can see the relationship between them,

Can you feel Chakras active in another person if you place your hand over the Chakra?

Can you relate to how chakras react to events in your life?

Can you understand and relate to how the interactions of the Chakras, determine how your various relationships express?

Have you tried projecting Universal Energy to another person?

Remember to write down the answers to these ponderings in your journal.

Let your mind offer up any other questions that might be applicable to these subject.

114

Developing a healthy mind-body relationship through mind management

Section 3

Managing Your Mind

Chapter 1

Introduction

Are you feeling stressed out?

Is life getting to be too much?

You are not alone. Stress is rampant throughout all levels of our society.

People are becoming seriously ill and dying prematurely because of excessive stress.

If you look in any library or do a search on the internet, you will find mountains of information on stress. These are some of the questions you will find:

- What causes it?
- What does it do to us?
- How does it affect our lives and our loved ones?
- What is stress?
- Is all stress harmful?

I ask you this-

How come, if we have all this information, are people still being struck down prematurely?

Why are people dying before their time from stressed-related diseases?

The Most Important Offering I have for you!!!

When stress is referred to in this book, it is not really the stress that is the concern, it is the attitudes and habits that promote and maintain stress, the reactions to stress that are of concern.

The stress of normal life is not bad for you; in fact, it is good for you. It reminds you that you are alive. It is the stress promoted through mismanagement of some of life's situations that causes noticeable deterioration of health and quality of life that is of concern.

In this section, we are going to take a very different look at stress. Different because my perspective says that living with stress is a choice, not a fact of life.

You have the choice to be stressed out or you can read this book and learn how to manage your life better, or at least manage it in a better way.

I promise you we will not reiterate the stories of old. I will not suggest to you to go to your doctor and get him to prescribe any of a thousand pills to cure you.

If you are currently under the care of a doctor, counselor, or any other health professional, please use this information as an assistant to their good work.

My intention is to provide good support for whatever method of healing you are doing. If it is working, please keep going.

My desire for you is to know that by reading and studying this information, you have gained a new understanding of how stress got to be a part of your life. My plan is to enlighten you about my truth about stress and to give you some simple techniques to get your life in order so that stress is what it is supposed to be, not what it currently is in your life.

Am I going to tell you that there will be no stress in your life? Absolutely not. The only time you will know a stress free time is after you have paid your bill and checked out of this great hotel.

What I am going to do is help you to understand how you create stress in your life and how you have let it take over without you even knowing. My goal is to give you back your life, your health, your relationships, and the joy of being alive on this planet.

So come on with me on the journey. Although the message is very serious, I will try to keep this light and fun. After all, this is the way life is supposed to be.

In this book, I try to be as unbiased as possible when providing you with what I feel is crucial information for you to know for managing your life. I am a free thinker. Although I certainly have my affiliations with organizations and schools I have studied with, my purpose in providing this information has no slant to it and no desire for you to conform to anything except of your choosing.

We now have the opportunity to take a different look at what we believe is true for us and make the necessary changes for our own benefit and for our descendants.

Chapter 2

Where Did It All Go Wrong?

Do you remember when you were a kid? Do you remember those great summer nights hanging around with your buds, not a care in the world?

What happened?

Life did!

All the time you were a child, although you may not have been aware of it, you were busy learning the rules of life. And like most people, those rules you learned way back before your wisdom teeth came in are still hard at work in your life today.

Psychologists say that 90% of the beliefs you have today were created before you saw your seventh birthday. Isn't that wonderful? So what were you doing before that glorious day?

How about some of these great pastimes?

- Getting beaten up by the neighborhood bully
- Watching mom and dad scream at each other.

- Learning the multiple uses of belts and straps every time you tried to experience life for yourself.
- Trying to get your parents' attention and approval so you could feel good about your life.
- Hiding from people who wanted to hurt you.
- Trying to develop new friendships every time mom and dad opted for a great new place to live.
- Skipping school

No matter what happened during childhood, each of us learned that life does not work out the way we thought it would in our mind.

I have often said that something went seriously wrong with my life the day that I was booking my trip on Star Trek's Holodeck computer. I thought I was punching in a long term holiday hanging out on the beach in Jamaica enjoying the Caribbean sunsets!

Did I get a rude awakening! I haven't even seen Jamaica this trip!

I finally realized not that long ago that it was not the Holodeck computer that screwed up.

It was my perception of life!

I was trying to run my life based on the rules I had learned as a kid!

The rules I had learned were not realistic for my life now and did nothing for me in helping me to manage my life optimally and healthily.

Of course, I was stressed out!

Could you imagine trying to bake a cake when the instructions you have are for making soup? It cannot and will not ever work no matter how hard you try!

That is the way we do so much of life! It's no wonder stress is so rampant. We are totally off kilter with our life because we keep trying to live our life based on inaccurate and inadequate information. How can we expect to create a wonderful life when many of the rules we base our life on are actually designed to sabotage us?

Do you think that maybe the same thing has happened to you… and likely everyone else?

Is it possible that we are still living on those same old rules that probably didn't even serve us when we were little? And for the most part, we don't even realize what they are doing to our lives. No wonder we are stressed out!

It is not possible to build a healthy lifestyle if we have unhealthy beliefs about ourselves and life in general.

Is there anything we can do about it? Is there any hope for us, or for mankind? Are we destined to evaporate as a species due to en masse burnout?

So where did it all go wrong?

Well, this is going to take the whole book to discuss this one. I must forewarn you though, I am a little radical in my view of the world and a whole lot jaded. I am not going to spend very much time explaining the basis of our belief systems as this book is a handbook to get your life back on track right now!

If you want to know more about core beliefs and how they impact your life, may I suggest you read my first book:

Embracing The Blend

What Mom And Dad Didn't Know

They Were Teaching You.

Anyway, somewhere back in time, someone thought it would be cute to promote the idea that we had to live our lives according to the demands and desires of other people and other things in our lives just so they could be happy and feel in control.

How many times have we heard that old classic line: "Do it for your mama?"

We bought into it well, so now we spend most of our time trying frantically to pay off mortgages bigger than the national debt of 1938, trying to make support payments for kids and spouses who couldn't take the stress anymore, and a gazillion other daily activities that have to be dealt with all in the name of living a successful life and keeping "mama" happy.

Then when we finally have a few minutes of downtime, we zone out by guzzling beer while drowning ourselves in some mindless TV shows filled with violence.

I ask you, where is there peace in that?

It's like living in a hamster cage. We get ourselves on that infernal wheel only getting off to feed, breed, and die.

If you look at how your parents lived, they never stopped working, did they? But who did they do it for?

In reality, they did it for themselves. But their rhetoric sounded something like this: "We did all this for you. We worked ourselves to the bone, so you could have the good life ... and on and on".

Recognition of this bit of nonsense is the first step in the realization of what went wrong.

We never do things for other people unless the action first has a benefit for ourselves at some level.

Often when people tell you that they are doing things for you, they are just applying a wonderful coating of guilt onto your belief systems as they attempt to keep you in their control. After all, they have become comfortable with who they see you as, so they will do anything to keep you there in an attempt to protect their comfort zone.

We have learned to live in a manner much like the way some caterpillars did in an experiment a while back. The scientist put a bunch of them around the rim of a glass. The caterpillars thought this was their lot in life, so they kept hanging onto the rim. Every time one of these characters started to fall off, their buddies on either end would pull them back up.

Sound familiar? How many times have you been pulled back into your rut by your family, friends, etc.?

What if you wanted your life to go somewhere different than they were comfortable with? What if you were to just let go?

The key to understanding what happened is this:

Somewhere along the line, we forgot what we came to this life for. We forgot about being here for the joy and the experience of being alive and free and to decide for ourselves what our life is for.

We traded this knowledge for "feeling safe" by giving away our power to anybody and anything that would take it.

We then covered ourselves even deeper in this muck by allowing our egos to take over our lives and make us believe that accumulating stuff and being bigger and richer than other people is what makes us great and powerful.

Sadly, all we have done is ruined a great time and seriously shortened our life spans.

So, are you with me?

I say we need to have a revolution!

We need to take back our power as individual people and in return, we can share the planet as the happy people we were meant to be.

127

128

It appears that we are suffocating under this illusion of "having to".

Chapter 3

What is all this stress doing to us?

We all have our own version of "Survivor" going on. I am not going to get into a bunch of boring statistics. You know what your life is like. No statistic in the world will accurately describe what motivated you to pick this book up.

Rather than numbers and boring statistics, this book is about reality living or more accurately, living in reality. The evidence is in our face, every day of our lives. We see the changes happening every time we breathe. Now we need to get back in charge of our lives or we also will be a statistic.

I feel like most people I see in my life are trying to just keep up with all the "stuff" that's going on. Life seems to be about "surviving" rather than living. It seems that life has become like a perpetual speedboat that keeps whipping us along so fast that we feel like we can't jump off for fear of being injured or even killed.

There is less and less time available for having fun, and generally relaxing. Without this downtime, our bodies and mind have no opportunity to recharge. Our boat is constantly at full speed ahead with little hope of changing course.

So what happens when we live a life of being continually on the go, pressing forward in a relentless effort to make others happy by constantly "doing"?

Later on, I will talk about the body aspect of stressful living. Right now, I would like us to focus on lifestyle concerns. Some of the great complaints about how we live at this time are directly related to this need for constant busyness and the resulting rising tide of stress. They include road rage, the increase in violent crime, emotional and psychological damage to our children, and, domestic violence, along with the increase in the number of divorces and much more.

Just medicate and go!

And of course, we need to look at what we are doing to Mother Earth. The increase in pollution and general stress on the planet due to our rising demand for consumer goods and the toll that our rising population has taken is a direct result of a planet of people who need to have that void filled from outside their being because they do not take the time to fill it themselves from within.

Have you noticed the drastic change in weather in the last few years? That is our demand for consumer products that is fueling it. No sense in blaming China and India for creating the pollution. If we didn't want the stuff, they wouldn't be making it!

We seem to be obsessed with the need to fill the void inside ourselves with "stuff" just so we can feel good, so we can believe we are successful. Now, I am not advocating that we all go live on communes and draw our water from wells and eat only carrots. I enjoy having a nice car and a beautiful home and lots of other nice things. But I am not willing to die for them! And I know that my survival is not dependent on having them!

It is not the possessions or the desire for them that is the concern; it is the attitude of having to have them to survive, that is the problem!

Let's look at our bodies. Much of the foods we eat are manufactured from chemicals rather than plant or animal matter. We microwave our food rather than either cooking it naturally or eating it raw. And to finish it off, we eat it so fast that the food gets broken down by adrenaline rather than digestive juices. Then, when our body retaliates, we pop pills to suppress the signals that tell us that things are going awry.

Is that stress causing?

The average person today gets their exercise from pushing either a pen or a computer mouse around all day followed by a healthy dose of pushing buttons on the television remote at night. Oh sorry, we must also include the elbow bending derived from slurping back several beers each evening.

Does that promote peace of mind?

The end result is obesity, high blood pressure, strokes, heart attacks, diabetes, cancer, and other diseases manifesting in a lot of unhappy people who die a lot younger than they need to.

Now is the time, in fact, the only time we really have to make the changes in our lives so we can live in a more healthy and functional manner.

133

Life is about making choices.

Chapter 4

What can we do about it?

We make some choices automatically and we make some through conscious effort.

Life has become so busy now that it seems there is no time for taking a break and making those deliberate choices. Every moment seems to require a new decision being made even though we haven't really decided on the last one yet.

Did you know that we process over double the amount of information today than our parents did at our age? We also live about twice the amount of life in a day than people did a hundred years ago.

It is not difficult to travel many thousands of miles in one day, today. A hundred years ago, most people barely lost sight of the town they were born in.

We need to accept that life is not the same as it was generations ago.

At the same time, we also need to understand that our psyche or the mental side of us has not adjusted to the so-called demands of this faster paced life. The result being adaptation to stress by synthetic means such as drugs and alcohol or working until we either have a mental breakdown or just plain old opt out of the game we call life.

I think one of the first things we need to realize is that most of us have taken on a whole lot more in our lives than our mind can comfortably handle.

We need to admit to ourselves that some things in our lives need to change. I feel we need to also realize that if we do not change them of our own volition, the force of life will change them for us.

We have grown up with a belief that we need to work tirelessly to prove our worth, to keep the image of our parents giving us approval in our heads placated. The truth is:

As adults, we are not obligated to do what others want, not even our parents. We have the right to choose for ourselves and create life according to our wants, needs, and desires.

The only thing we need to do is give ourselves some space to breathe once in a while as we are living our lives.

Just stop and take a breath once in a while!

It is also good for each of us to recognize the noise in our head we carry with us that drives us into that state of being out of control. We have become adrenaline junkies. We live to the extreme. We use the "extremeness" of our lifestyle to justify staying unconscious, running from that never-ending voice. As long as we can hold onto this "drug", we can avoid ourselves and our own responsibility for our own lives.

Unfortunately, this would be like continuing to joy ride in a speedboat that has already struck a big rock out in the middle of a lake.

Here are some examples of what I mean:

- We persistently drive our cars too fast.
- We drink gallons of coffee when we know we are already "wired".
- We get upset and aggressive when other people don't agree with us.
- We constantly have to have the "latest and greatest" whether we need it or not.
- We watch violent television programs.
- Our life goal is to be "Number One".
- We live in "perpetual motion" (even in our sleep)
- We think that if we stop, so will our life.
- And oh yes, welcome to the 21st Century… we have to check our cell phones every five minutes even after we retire to sleep, just in case!

In my mind, the whole process of so-called "normal" living has gone berserk. We have lost any ability to manage our lives effectively. And, we dare to call it living the good life!

What can we do about it?

The first thing we can do is realize that we always have choices.

We can continue to drive the boat right down to the bottom of the lake and drown or we can get to shore and fix it before continuing.

There is no such thing as "have to". We always have choices. It is a matter of whether we will make our choice by rote and carry on as we always have or will we stop and choose to try something different (Hopefully before life forces our hand!).

If we continue making the same decisions, we will eventually go down with the boat.

If we decide to choose a different outcome, we are faced with a dilemma, and this is where the fear arises that keeps most people in their rut.

"What if I make the wrong decision?" you ask.

Well my friend, would you rather risk making a decision that turns out badly but differently, or just continue making the same old choice again and again?

In a worst-case scenario, you make a decision that still takes you down with the boat, but at least you now know you have tried something different. That alone is a win.

Life is a gamble... but the risk can be limited.

If you take the time to think about what you would like the outcome to be rather than just allowing knee jerk reactions, it is quite likely you will make a decision that is not detrimental. It will likely need fine tuning as the situation rises again or develops. Just know and accept that it will not hurt you if you have made a deliberate and conscious decision that is different from your old habitual choice.

Let's look at the first steps in understanding what you can do about getting some control in this stressful life you have created for yourself. They are:

- Recognize that you are living beyond your manageable limits.

- Recognize that you can create a life that is simpler and more manageable simply by making the choice to change your life and by implementing what you determine is necessary to integrate the change.

As we progress, you will learn several other concepts and tools that will help you retool your life so you can manage your life in a manner that supports the life you really desire.

139

140

How we do stress is a learned process!

Chapter 5

How did we learn to do stress?

Everything we have learned in this life has been ingested through watching and interacting with others. In my book *Embracing The Blend, What Mom And Dad Didn't Know They Were Teaching You,* I go into much greater detail about the mechanics of how we learn.

For the sake of the simplicity and brevity of this handbook, suffice it to say that we have learned virtually everything we know and all the ways we react to life by watching others.

If you watch a father and son walking down the street, you will notice that they most likely walk in a similar gait. This is because our children learn to walk by watching other people around them walking. The person they feel most similar to or have the strongest affinity with will be the person they emulate in much of what we consider automatic learning.

The son actually learns the process of walking by watching the others around him, and then eventually learns to get up and walk on his own by repeating their actions.

The same thing can be said for how we deal with life situations. If you look at the authority figures (mom, dad, teachers, siblings, etc.) in your life and how they have made their choices in various situations, and then look at how you do things, you will likely see a common pattern.

This is because most people unconsciously learn "the functional method" for dealing with a certain situation and then by copying it. This is done completely without any conscious thinking at all!

Some common examples of this could be:

- The language we speak.
- The words we use to express ourselves, especially in certain situations.
- Body gesturing or automatic reactions to certain stimuli
- Activities used to fill your days (television, sports, reading, etc.).
- Use of alcohol and drugs
- Driving habits and how we deal with driving situations.
- The expression or suppression of emotions
- How we treat other people, especially children and people of the opposite sex.

Take a few moments now and look back at your childhood. Think of situations where your caregivers and role models acted out specific situations in their lives. After you have chosen a few scenarios look at how you react in those same situations. Who did you pattern yourself after?

Unless you have made some deliberate choices related to certain situations to change how you express your reaction to them, you can almost always pin your reaction as a copy of one of your caregivers. This is unconscious learning, and worse, unconscious expression.

This is also true of how we have learned to deal with stress.

As children, we literally know nothing about how to deal with life. Our unconscious mind is completely open to suggestions. We watch mom and dad deal with life. Life is one never-ending continuum of learning. Stress and dealing with stressful activities in life had no different consideration than learning how to use a toilet or eating with a fork or spoon. The mind does not care about the quality of the information, or even what the information is, it only wants information to fill the void.

When reactions to situations repeat again and again over a long period of time, they become engrained as an acceptable and automatic response to the given situation. This is true even if the result is not beneficial or acceptable to the authority figures or the individual committing the act.

It is really a sad state of affairs when a parent punishes a child for their reaction to a situation when all the child did was copy the parent in their own reaction, and yet it happens time and again, and will continue to recur until conscious change occurs.

But fear not, there is hope!

Learning how stress feels in your body is one of the basic tools for managing it.

Chapter 6

What does stress feel like?

One of the first steps in being able to deal with stress and managing it, is learning how to recognize how stress feels.

It is amazing how so many people today are not truly in touch with the feel of their body and its reactions as it works its way through each day. They are so wrapped up in reacting to life in their own unconscious patterns that they have lost any sense of connection to themselves, and therefore, do not realize the results until it is too late.

The result of long-term disconnection from body awareness is a premature breakdown at some or all levels. This might include physically, mentally, and/or emotionally. In the end, this person will be less than fully functional, or even dead.

Things one can look forward to by remaining in this unconscious process might include:

- Extreme mental fatigue causing an inability to think clearly, or at all.
- Mental or emotional breakdowns
- Pretty well any disease
- Uncontrolled outbursts of destructive emotions

- Loss of quality relationships with others
- Lack of true quality lifestyle
- A much shorter life

It is important to be able to recognize the symptoms that indicate stress is active or may be sitting on the sidelines waiting for the opportunity to activate in your life.

I know I promised that I would not get too academic in this book, but I feel it is important to understand how stress changes the body functions. I will try to keep it interesting while we tread through these puddles of academia.

Stress is a product of fear.

Fear produces changes in the body that are managed by the Endocrine System. The Endocrine System is composed of any of the glands that manufacture and/or distribute hormones. Hormones are not only found in the sex glands. Hormones are chemicals that cause changes to the functioning of your body due to any stimulus, often from an external source.

Adrenaline is a perfect example of what I am talking about. Another one is Insulin.

When a person feels unsafe, their glands produce and excrete hormones in order to excite certain functions in the body, so the body is prepared to either fight or run. This is called the "Fight or Flight" Syndrome.

Early recognition is essential to managing the situations in your life.

When a situation invokes stress, the body reacts in much the same way as when it is in fear mode. As you live each of your days, try to gain a better sense of the feelings of being in the current emotion, especially when you are feeling stress.

Due to the pace most of us live today, we continually find ourselves in a level of stress that is beyond the normal condition in which our body functions best at. Therefore, it takes far less to cause an unhealthy reaction.

These are some of the most common physical symptoms:

- Muscle tightness anywhere in the body that is not required for completing the current action, such as tight head muscles causing a headache, or back pains.
- Pulsing at the end of the nose and/or tingly lips
- Acidy stomach
- Inability to sit or stand still.
- Inability to think clearly, fast-moving mind that shifts from one thought to another in very fast rotation.
- Difficulty in breathing (Tight chest)
- Rapid heartbeat even though not exercising.
- Lots of gas from the digestive system
- Tingling hands
- In extreme cases, blurred vision

Mental and Emotional Symptoms include:

- An urgent feeling of needing to protect oneself.
- A feeling of panic
- A sense of feeling overwhelmed
- Inability to let go of a particular thought that keeps recycling in the mind.

These symptoms are commonly experienced when a person is feeling excessive stress. I strongly urge again to be aware of these feelings and of other feelings in the body that feel uncomfortable so that you can take appropriate action while they are still manageable and well before they can cause any damage.

Use these symptoms as a bridge to help you to recognize you have an opportunity to make a change.

We learned to react to life in this manner.

We can retrain ourselves to live differently.

When we learn to listen to our body, then do something about the messages; we can make our lives more happy, free and joyful!

150

**Stress is a learned reaction;
it is very manageable.**

Chapter 7

Mind Management is Stress Management

Now we get down to the business at hand, the reason I put this book together.

The first step in learning to manage stress in your life is realizing and accepting that you have a choice every time you "get stressed out".

You have the choice of whether to react in that unconscious manner or to respond differently.

The difference, by the way, between "react" and "respond" is the difference between acting out of habit and consciously making a choice.

Learning to manage stress in your life needs to start in the times when you are not feeling stressed.

If you understand well how to manage stress when you are feeling comfortable, it will be much easier for you to manage your life when situations fall apart.

Recognizing the effects of thoughts in your head is absolutely required. This requires being able to separate yourself from the outcome or the reaction. After all,

You are not your thoughts, and they are not you.

Being able to differentiate between who you are and the "things" going on in your life is essential for improving your mind and life management skills.

Please understand that you can not and will never ever have complete control over the events in your life. If you can get your head around this one fact, you will reduce stress in your life immeasurably.

In fact, if it be truly known, there is no such thing as control! In my understanding of the word "control", it presumes that there is an ability to understand and manage every aspect of a given situation all the time.

If that is not an ego-based definition, I do not know one!

Even if you look at a "control" valve on a plumbing system, this valve cannot comprehend or mitigate some action in the system that it has no knowledge of. Oops, where did that leak come from? Until it becomes aware of the problem it will do nothing. When it becomes aware, the best it can do is MANAGE!!!

It is the same in our lives. People who think they can control others to make their lives safe are en route to the bottom of the lake. If you are one of them, are you ready to become aware of how you manage your life?

Are you willing to make a change?

Exercises

So, this is where the exercises begin. For your benefit I have also provided these exercises on my website:

https://powerfulyoupowerfulme.com

Please read through this section first before doing the exercises.

Conscious Mind Management

Living In Present Time

Quieting The Mind

Sit yourself down, get comfortable and begin to relax. Sit with your hands unclasped on your lap and your feet relaxed and flat on the floor.

An important note: when you breathe, whether now or anytime, remember to breathe moving your abdominal muscles. This allows your lungs to refresh all of the air in them including at the base of the lungs.

If this does not occur, stale air stays in the bottom of the lungs and is redistributed through the blood causing a lack of revitalization (which increases stress).

As you settle in, take in three very slow easy deep breaths.

Now pretend there is a warm yellow sun beaming down on you from above your head. As you continue to breathe in a very slow deliberate manner, feel the warmth of the sun flowing down into your body.

Feel it flow down your head, your neck, into your chest, down into your abdomen, and down your legs, flowing right down into your feet and out into the earth below you.

Take your time and let yourself relax.

Feel your feet firmly planted on the ground. Focus on this feeling for a good moment, then let your consciousness move back up your body through your feet, up your legs into your pelvic region, up into your abdomen, through your chest, into your neck, and up to the top of your head and back up to your yellow sun.

Once you have done this action as many times as you desire, allow yourself to relax fully into your chair and feel the connection between you and the chair.

Focus on your breaths and the feeling of being in your body. Let yourself feel every part of your body from head to toe. Allow yourself to enjoy the feeling.

Every time you catch yourself thinking about something else, gently pull yourself back into focusing on your body and breath.

This is practicing being in the NOW. Feeling the sensations of being in your body, along with giving attention to your breath is a route for maintaining contact with present time.

Allow yourself to be aware of any feelings in your body. Make allowances for any sounds and smells in the room and just let them be. They belong in the present. Thoughts that distract your practice do not belong, so gently dismiss them.

Most important, be easy on yourself. Let yourself relax. When you are ready to finish up, just take a nice easy breath and open your eyes.

Practice this exercise every day. Practice it when you are feeling calm. Teach yourself to remember how it feels to be conscious of your body and breath in present time. This provides you with an anchor for when the times are hectic.

Keeping your mind present in the now allows you to choose to stay out of old habits and makes a space for you to make better decisions.

Remember, when you take the time to make good decisions for yourself, the results are good for others in the long run.

Good decisions also make a peaceful mind.

157

Stress is a result of poor management of your thoughts.

Chapter 8

Managing Your Thoughts

Definitely the biggest challenge in keeping yourself managed and at peace is dealing with the noise in your head. Fortunately, there are several key pieces of information available that will help you to gradually take the driver's seat in mind management.

Definitely practicing the exercise in the previous chapter is a basic part of creating change in your life and gaining more peace of mind.

Next is understanding that stress is a choice.

You see, most people do not understand that thoughts are manageable. The mind is no different than any other tool. The only difference is that we are not generally taught that we can do anything about stress or anything else that goes on in our head except tolerate it or medicate it. As you will soon understand, neither of these solutions is necessary in ordinary circumstances.

Please realize and accept:

> **You are not your mind, your thoughts, or your ego.**

These three are only tools that are implanted inside your being for your benefit. As such, their function and purpose are commonly and severely misunderstood. Let me explain.

Your mind is a very powerful tool. In fact, computers are designed after our brain/mind relationship and work exactly the same way. Like computers, the mind can be turned off and on at will… and the information in it can be managed. It just takes practice.

Your thoughts are the information processed by your mind.

Thoughts by themselves have no power.

Thoughts require input from your emotional body in order to activate.

Generally, thoughts that promote stress are just rehashed thoughts from your childhood dressed up as adults. They likely were not based on correct information when you were a child and are still just as erroneous today. However, they are the information your mind (computer) knows and therefore bases its reactions on.

In many therapies today, the desire is either to have the client work through the emotional upheaval or medicate to suppress the thoughts. The process you have been provided with allows you to turn the undesirable thoughts off by taking away their power. You will also learn to give more "juice" to beneficial thoughts. This is the basis of what I call mind management. Off with the "bad" and on with the "good".

Your ego is one of the most misdirected organs in your body. We are conditioned to believe, in this society, that we are our egos. We do not differentiate between who we truly are and the persona we see through our ego. Because of this belief, the ego is given far more power than it is due.

The ego is an important part of our total self, but it is no more important than any other organ in our body. It has a specific purpose just like the brain, liver, kidneys, etc.

The purpose of the ego is to carry our identity around and to be the base of our intuition for survival. It is like our cyber-wallet so if today you are Susie, tomorrow you do not wake up believing you are George. Your ego keeps things straight!

In days of old when we needed to rely on our intuition, we needed to have a good awareness of everything going on around us. If we didn't, we could quickly become an involuntary part of the food chain.

The ego's purpose is to protect us, to keep us alive. The ego is found in the subconscious mind. It has no ability to discern right from wrong. It only knows what it knows. It tries to regulate its owner's life according to what it "knows". Unfortunately, this information is often wrong.

What I am trying to tell you is this:

Much of the stress in your life is caused by your subconscious mind trying to make your life conform to its perception of life.

How unrealistic is that?

Is your life the same as it was when you were six years old? Of course, it isn't! Did you really understand the full scope of life when you were six? Did those beliefs even serve you well as a child? Of course not! Usually, they just happened... and got you into more trouble... and they are likely still getting you into trouble!

So what can you do about it?

Learn to manage your mind.

As I said before, thoughts have no power unto themselves. You have to give them power for them to activate. This is generally an automatic unconscious process. But it does not have to be. You have free choice!

Here is an exercise that is vital in taking back your ability to effectively manage your life. Remember, these visualizations have been uploaded onto my website for your use.

(http://powerfulyoupowerfulme.com/videos/)

Do the exercise from the previous chapter to start with, and then bring your focus to the feeling of being in your body along with your breath. These are the anchors you use for staying in present time.

The next step is to allow a thought which stimulates stress to surface in your mind.

Allow yourself to feel how the thought affects you. Let your mind travel throughout your body determining how the thought has impacted any part.

Can you feel certain muscles being held tight? Do you feel any anxiety? How is your breathing? What is happening in your mind? Are there any other changes from your normal peaceful condition?

Now focus again on your breathing. Slowly take long breaths giving all of your attention to the breath. Remember how it felt to be fully in your relaxed body. Follow the breathing pattern back into the peaceful body.

Allow your mind to go into a stress-related thought again, and then follow your breathing back into peace and relaxation. You are making the conscious choice to move out of one thought into another.

If you are a visual person, this is the technique.

Imagine a chair in the back of your head. It is facing towards your forehead. Sit down in the chair. At the front of your head is a white screen like a movie theatre screen.

As you are sitting in the chair, allow your thoughts to appear on the screen. Try to watch them much like you are watching a movie. Try not to become engaged with the thoughts.

As a stressful thought comes up, melt it like an ice cream cone in the heat of summer. Each time the thought comes up, melt the thought again. Really get into the picture by letting the ice cream melt all over your hands. No licking!

Release your emotional connection to it so that the thought flies away.

Using either of these processes allows you to regain control over your thoughts. This is mind management. You are becoming your boss. With practice, you will be able to neutralize any thought you choose, so that you can maintain the level of management you desire.

This is the basis of having the use of the powerful mind you were born with. All you have to do is keep putting the garbage out!

One benefit of learning the neutralizing technique is that you can allow your mind to come to rest, even to the point where your mind will not have any thought in it at all.

The mind has a much larger tool kit inside it, if only we will open the box !

Chapter 9

The Power of Mind Management

Now that you have the ability and the power to delegate power to whichever thoughts you choose, you can take this to an even higher level.

This next step allows you to stimulate the higher, more desirable thoughts in a similar process to the neutralizing one in the last chapter.

Why would you want to do this?

Nature abhors a void and so does your mind. The ultimate outcome of this process is to have your mind doing exactly what you desire.

Therefore we must look at the elimination or neutralizing of the stressful thoughts as only one aspect of totally conditioning your mind.

This effect may only last for a few seconds at first but as you practice and become okay with not having to be constantly thinking, your mind will remain in this state of passiveness for several moments or longer.

In yogic terms, this is the state of Nirvana, total peace.

In this space, your mind is not inactive or stopped, it is only resting. In this space, you leave room for rejuvenation and inspiration. It is vital to your health and progress on your life journey.

As you practice these exercises, allow yourself the pleasure of enjoying the quiet. It is truly one of the greatest gifts we can give ourselves today.

These exercises, by the way, only need to take 5-10 minutes. They should be done regularly at least once per day. However, in stressful times, please stop and go into the quiet as often as necessary until you can maintain a reasonable level of calm.

Please note that these exercises are designed to help you live life more fully. They are not meant as an escape from responsibility.

Life will continue to present challenging times, and in some cases, it will seem like a never-ending barrage. By learning to anchor yourself from within and manage your mind, you will be able to develop a much healthier approach to moving through the issues as they express in your life.

Once the emotion has been removed from the thoughts, you will soon be able to view them in a detached manner and learn what the basis of the thought pattern is, so that you can deal with the message rather than the onslaught of the emotional riptide.

It is part of being human that we have these emotional upheavals. The purpose of this program is to provide you with tools to move through them more quickly, to return yourself to calmness.

Accepting that these situations occur now and will occur again in the future is part of the flavor of life and will make it much easier to ride them through.

Now, onto the next part of the exercise.

As I said before, there needs to be balance in the mind management process, therefore we need to counter the neutralizing of the undesirable, stress-related thoughts.

This is done by reinforcing the desirable thoughts.

Mind management has two components:

Neutralize the undesirable and reinforce the desirable.

So let's learn how to reinforce the desirable.

Again, close your eyes and relax by taking a few slow, deep breaths. This time choose a thought that you deem to be desirable. It could be something you desire or even just a feeling of well-being, or it could be a picture of someone or something you have in your life that brings you feelings of gratitude or joy.

Feel how you feel as you allow this thought to permeate your mind. What changes in your body do you feel? How is your breathing?

If you are a visual, you can repeat the process in your head with the chair and the blank screen. This time, however, you choose a desirable thought. Allow it to come up on the screen. Keep it there, enjoy it.

Now, project energy from your heart to the thought. Revel in the joy of having what you see on the screen.

Decide for yourself what emotion you wish to attach to this thought. Send this emotion into the thought and allow yourself to really enjoy the connection.

Next, and most important, is to own the feelings you have created. Allow them to exist in your life in PRESENT tense. Allow yourself to enjoy them, embellish them and make them grow. The more intensity in the feeling, the more your mind will remember it.

No matter what the positive thought, you must attach emotion to it so that the subconscious mind learns to know the experience of positively injected emotions and feelings. By regularly practicing this process, your mind will be reconditioned to feed on positive, desirable energy rather than the old stuck low energy it formerly knew that promotes stress.

This process will retrain the mind to search for and accept positive, healthy energy. This stimulates the endocrine system in a beneficial manner.

It is important to understand that your mind needs to be fed and will always be fed through the energy you attract into your body through your thinking. By focusing on and learning to manifest positive, stimulating energy through focused thought, you create a life that is more dynamic, resourceful, abundant, and healthy.

Although activities that stimulate old memories are unavoidable in life, it is how you choose to allow them to impact your present time through your emotions that makes the difference.

You can choose to allow the unconscious mind to wreak havoc in your life and bowl over your health and dreams or you can take charge by reconditioning your mind so that you have conscious management over the programming... and the outcomes.

There are no instances in life where you cannot maintain some level of choice through mind management.

Remember that it has taken you all of your life so far to learn to react to stress in the old way, it will take practice and time to instill this new way of responding to life's influences.

All you have to do is remember yourself and remember you always have a choice in how you let outside influences affect your life.

And most important:

    Always remember to be your own best friend.

As you retrain your mind, give yourself the space to adjust to the new way.

Appreciate yourself for making the effort on a continuing basis.

Love yourself for the wonderful being that you are.

Learn to know the joy of feeling the feeling of being you in your own energy and vitality.

By making this effort for yourself, you are helping to make the world a better place to live for everyone. Now we can more easily relate and participate in the concept of Powerful You, Powerful me.

After all, the greatest source of power you can participate in is by empowering another person, while not disempowering yourself.

Ponderings

Some of these questions may be challenging for you to think about, but they may be useful tools for re-thinking how you use stress in your life.

How does stress affect your daily life?

Does it affect your health?

Is the way you use stress in your life a tool you use for protection in uncomfortable situations in some situations?

Is stress stopping you from moving forward in your life?

Can you relate the way you stress out to a role model from your childhood?

How did you use stressing out as a tool for manipulation when you were a child? Who did you need to protect yourself from?

Are you willing to make changes so you can allow yourself to feel safe?

Would being more open and vulnerable in your life be valuable to you?

How would these changes make your life appear different?

What benefits would you gain from it?

Who else in your life would gain from your positive changes?

175

Being A parent is one of the most rewarding tasks we can take on as human beings.

Once it starts though, it is a full time life commitment.

Section 4

Parenting

The most important and most rewarding job we ever have.

Please check out my website for free tools for change

www.powerfulyoupowerfulme.com

Chapter 1

Introduction

Children are undeniably our most important asset, for without them our species will not continue to flourish.

Since we first arrived on this planet, we have borne children, raised them and made more... and yet... we still do not really understand why we have them or what we are supposed to do with them once we have them.

Since time immemorial, we have propagated our species without really understanding even the basics of the whys and whats of bearing these little bundles of joy.

It just seems to be a process we do on default !

Fortunately, our species and society in general have now evolved to the point where we are sophisticated enough and have enough space in our lives to learn the real truth about why we have children and how we can make the best out of the greatest thing we can create in our lives.

The purpose of this section of this book is not to give you rules about how to raise your child to be the best child on the block or how to discipline your child. The purpose of this book is for you to understand the three most important aspects of raising your child that will help you support them in realizing their potential as their most amazing selves.

All human beings are amazing, just in the fact that they have been created. They just need to know it and learn to continually grow with it in the most functional manner.

Although we may not always agree about the fundamental techniques used to raise our children, there are only really three things our kids truly need.

180

Understanding who you are is the first step in raising amazing children!

Chapter 2

Who Are You?

Have you ever stopped to ask yourself this question?

Who are you?

How do you the answer this question?

There are no wrong answers here. You can believe you are whomever you choose to be.

However, there are likely some answers that are better than others. In this chapter, we will start by exploring ourselves and how we perceive ourselves as we live out our lives.

Do you notice these days, no matter where we choose to live, we regularly see many people who are absolutely obsessed with photographing themselves. You may even be one of them! It does not matter what they are doing, there needs to be a regimen of pictures detailing every step.

The "Selfie" era is well upon us. Click! Click! Click! How many times have you observed people photographing themselves again and again, as they move through their day?

Every time they do something they consider worth noting, there goes another picture. It is a wonder they don't run out of film!

And then they post them on Social Media expecting adoration from their thousands of "friends" who are also Selfie addicts.

Why are these people caught up in this craze?

Another popular craze is "Monday Night Football". These people see their world as an extension of the drama that unfolds as their favorite team marches through the season. These people often find the ups and downs of their life based on how well their team is doing.

So what happens at the end of the season? What happens to the lives of these individuals who see their life expression as a reflection of Monday Night Football?

There are hundreds of other activities that occur in people's lives that help them shape who they think they are.

And what about people who are so engrossed in their careers that they know no other way of identifying themselves? Who are they without their job?

So, I ask again, who are you? How do you define yourself?

When we are asked to tell something about ourselves and our lives, the normal answer is to paraphrase or sum up the events that have occurred to us as we have lived our adventure.

I am a man, a carpenter, I drive an Audi, I have two children, I go to such and such church, and I live in ...

When people identify themselves through photographs, their favorite team on Monday Night Football, their jobs, etc.... they are using external identification.

The truth is that when a person uses outside attributes as their identifier, they are blocking their own ability to know themselves.

The reason for this is that when we ask the question "Who am I?", once an answer is posted, the questioning is usually satisfied, and no other investigation is needed.

Have you ever tried asking yourself a question that you do not know the answer to? Doesn't your mind automatically answer, "I don't know!" I rest my case!

What we need to understand in investigating our answer to the question is... We are not part of the outside world... we are inside this body we carry around with us!

Nothing that one can see identifies who we are, they just tell the story of how we are doing our life. Can you see the difference?

No matter what or who you are, it is likely that this is what an introductory conversation will look like:

"Hi! I am Bob. I live in Langley. I drive a bus. I like to golf. I am married with 6 kids."

Then the other person gets their turn.

"Hi! I am Bjorn. I live in Oslo. I am a fisherman. I have two kids from my first marriage and inherited six more in my second."

After the one person has gone through their list of attributes, hopefully the other person will get to do so as well and voila! We are on the road to a relationship!

Based on What?

How we develop relationships is often based on how we perceive ourselves and what our emotional needs are at the time of the first interaction... and how we react to the information provided by the other person. Once the glue has dried, the relationship is on. This is usually where politics or something emotionally engaging kicks in, so each individual can test out the commonalities of the other. The more agreements each one has with the other, the more likely they will from a bond.

Then what?

What is the primal purpose of this relationship? How does this relationship fit into your life and what does it do for you or the other person?

There are many people and many types of relationships that flow through the average person's life. Each of them is different and they each serve a different purpose in the overall puzzle that expresses as this individual and their life.

Have you ever stopped to analyze what purpose any of the relationships you personally have, serve in your life?

Most people just accept that these relationships are a part of their life, some here for the long run and some just in the now, without ever stopping to ask what importance this person is for them in their overall life plan. They don't try to find out what this person represents to them.

Why does it matter?

There are a lot of questions that can be asked about the basic operations of our lives and our relationships. If you are a person who seeks to know yourself, you likely have already asked many of these questions. The answering of these continuing questions may take a whole life time… or more. As one question is answered, another question arises.

So, let's get back to the original question. Who are you?

How you answer this question forms the basis for how you structure your life and how well you truly know yourself.

If you believe you are identified through the "things" that exist in your life, then you will likely be a person who chases those things. What is that old adage?

> "The one with the most toys at the end wins!"

Life will be a never ending race for collecting things: Homes, cars, trophy spouses, hobby paraphernalia, money and such. There will never be enough.

Some people are actually skilled enough in this game to be able to manage the void they feel through the drive to accumulate stuff, while others will spend their lives chasing a car that goes too fast, leaving them a wreck on the side of the road in life.

Others will choose to avoid the game and live a rather austere life of mediocrity, safe from the gamble that fuels the race. They live in constant dissatisfaction, believing that they were handed the "short straw" in life.

Until people who believe they are what they possess or don't possess, come to a more realistic understanding of how to truly identify themselves, they will likely never find true satisfaction in their lives.

187

The true answer to the question "who are you?" is not found in the external world. No one can find themselves in their collection of or the avoidance of things.

We are much greater than all the things of the outside world.

The true answer to the question "Who are you?" is:

I am.

"I am" is a complete statement on its own.

If you add anything onto this powerful two word statement, you have just created a limitation for yourself.

If today you claim to be a carpenter, but tomorrow you find yourself working as a medical doctor, are you not still the same person?

If you identify yourself by a medical condition, what if you were miraculously cured, do you become somebody else?

Any aspect of how we identify ourselves based on what we perceive in the outer world is a limitation!

We are not our job, our gender, our sexual preference, our ethnicity, our nationality, our body, our religion or any other external aspect we express.

These outer manifestations are just expressions of this particular life our soul has chosen so we can fulfill the needs of our life purpose.

The only correct answer is... I am!

Knowing yourself for who you really are is absolutely essential!

Chapter 3

Hello, Here I am!

Let's start with an exercise!

A couple important notes first:
1. **When you breathe, whether now or anytime, remember to breathe moving your abdominal muscles. This allows your lungs to refresh all of the air in them including at the base of the lungs. If this does not occur, stale air stays in the bottom of the lungs and is redistributed through the blood causing a lack of revitalization (which increases stress).**
2. **Although it is called visualizing you can complete it using whatever sense you like. Most important is that you believe you are actually doing it, and, it is working for you. Use your imagination!**

Seat yourself somewhere comfortable and allow yourself to relax. Sit with your hands unclasped on your lap and your feet relaxed and flat on the floor.

As you settle in, take in three very slow easy deep breaths making sure you allow your abdominal muscles to help.

Now, pretend there is a warm yellow sun beaming down on you from above your head. As you continue to breathe in a very slow deliberate manner, feel the warmth of the sun flowing down into your body.
Feel it flow down into your head, your neck, into your chest, down into your abdomen and down your legs, flowing right down through your feet and into the earth below you.

Take your time and let yourself relax. Remember to keep breathing.

Feel your feet firmly planted on the ground like the roots of a tree. Focus on this feeling for a good moment, then let your consciousness move back up your body through your feet, up your legs into your pelvic region, up into your abdomen, through your chest, into your neck and up to the top of your head and back up to your yellow sun.

Once you have done this action as many times as you desire, allow yourself to relax fully into your chair with no focus but to feel the connection between you and the chair, just letting yourself relax.

Focus on your breaths again and the feeling of being in your body. Let yourself feel every part of your body from head to toe. Allow yourself to enjoy the feeling.

If your mind gets in the way, just stop, relax, focus on taking a deep breath for a moment and let the thought go... and relax.

When you are ready, take a nice deep breath and open your eyes as you exhale.

You have just said hello to your true self!

As we discussed in Chapter 1, you are not all the stuff that follows "I am".

They are just a distraction from the true reality of who you are.

They are only expressions of what you have done with your time or pieces of the package you were given to create your physical appearance.

Now that you have met your true self, please take the time regularly to visit. You have a lot to catch up on!

So why is it important to commune with your inner self?

Once you know the feeling of what you feel like, you can use it to determine what is real and what is not. Your inner voice will have the opportunity, as you practice, to give you messages through feelings that relate to what you do to express yourself as your life moves on.

When we focus on external activities, especially if we are obsessed with them like needing to take selfies a dozen times a day, we avoid creating and maintaining a clear relationship with ourselves. We also find ourselves much more stressed because we lack an anchor to help us base our life on.

When we are able to feel our true selves, we begin to see and understand the facades we have used that prevent us from connecting with ourselves. Memories of many events that have occurred in our lives are held in our subconscious mind that misrepresent who we truly are.

When these events are tied to strong emotions, the binding is just like cement. Issues of abuse and neglect, for example, are strong identifiers that hold us to our past and beliefs that prevent us from expressing in clarity the amazing person we really are.

Persons who struggle with such strong beliefs may find it challenging to focus on the exercise above. The ego, which has been given the job as our great protector, does not want to let this person go anywhere it is uncomfortable with, so it creates distractions to keep them away.

However, with patience and persistence, and by focusing on the feeling of intentionally relaxing and letting yourself feel good while relaxing, the stranglehold can be gradually released.

The ego is not the enemy in this process; it is just doing its job. It just needs to be retrained! It has been running the show for a very long time on what is likely incorrect information it learned when you were a child.
One of the ego's jobs is to keep us safe. It does this by collecting memories that have shaped our personal perception of our lives.

It then very quickly analyzes current events to determine if they might feel similar to any of those past events and sets up protective devices to "stop the pain" of remembering when necessary.

This can cause a great deal of discomfort for the person in the present tense, especially for those who have suffered dearly at the hands of others, because they cannot see the world around them beyond the memories. They just keep reliving new events as reflections of the old, while reliving the pain.

The key point in doing this exercise is to not allow yourself to get involved with thoughts that come up. Just recognize the memory is only a thought, and let it go by focusing on the energy of the sun flowing into you, and your breathing. Eventually, the thought will evaporate, and you can carry on without it.

If necessary you can try journaling on the thought if it is a really insistent one, but be very cautious that you do not reinforce the thought. The goal is to relax and let yourself be who you truly are!

Once you get really good at it, you will be able to dismiss the thoughts quickly and return your focus to the good feeling.

This process does not change your past, but it will certainly change your present and future, as the ego will eventually accept your new program when it realizes the old method of protection does not serve you anymore.

Please understand that this process is not a replacement for counselling. If there are past issues that are still clouding your freedom of expression, please get help. If anything, this process will assist you in your healing and help you change your life.

Be sure to inform your counselor about this work you are doing through the information provided in this booklet, so they can help you more in making changes while utilizing this process.

Once you gain some proficiency in this process, you will realize that you are not your thoughts, or your past memories and you will no longer need to feel that you have to hang onto them. You will have begun your true healing journey.

It is also important to realize that every person on this planet has some memories that cause them to have a tainted perception of their true possibilities.

We are not the only ones who have suffered. In this, it is always best to realize that we are all works in progress and need to be handled carefully and respectfully, especially as we begin to reveal new thoughts, and come to experiences our true selves.

196

Karma is just the law of Cause and Effect

It is neither good nor bad.

It just is!

Chapter 4
Karma

Did you know there is more to life than you can actually see?

Many people have a hard time understanding and accepting this statement. I think this is because there is a certain kind of safety in being able to actually use only one's physical senses to determine if something is real.

Fortunately, whether one believes it or not there is an invisible side to life. The great thing about this side of us is that it operates whether we choose to give it recognition or not.

Have you ever thought about what attracted you to a person like your mate or some other person who you just had to know and maybe be with?

That attraction is caused by your invisible side reacting to their invisible side.

I am only going to touch on this subject briefly here, as we have already spoken about karma extensively in a previous section. However, the most important aspect I want to share with you is that we do have both an invisible self and a visible self.

Inside the visible self, there are drives that help us to choose situations and people that we either need to attract into our lives or we need to help create, so they can fulfill their (and possibly our) life plan. These belong to the invisible self.

In order to properly help create these bundles of joy according to their long-term needs, they need to choose the right parents in the right situation. This is the beginning of the story; we call Karma and... dare I say... it begins a while before birth.

For example, I recall a dream I had when my wife was pregnant with our son. We had decided his first and second name but could not decide which order. In the dream, I saw my son climb up the outside of our house into our second story window and announce to me the order of his names, then he popped out the window and was gone.

We named him exactly as he instructed!

We are not going to go all Ayurvedic or Hindu or anything here, when explaining this understanding, even though the origins of the word "Karma" are found in these systems.

Very simply Karma is a system of cause and effect.

There are many layers to Karma though. It is not just a thing that happens when you do something bad. It is way more complex than that, but I will try to keep it fairly simple.

The karma we most readily recognize is Personal Karma. Some people are continually conscious of doing things right or wrong because they don't want to create Karma.

The reality is we are constantly creating Karma, because we live in a world of cause and effect.

When we tie up our shoes correctly, we don't fall down. Good Karma… Shoe lace comes undone, and we trip on it and fall, bad Karma.

There are two layers of Karma that are important to focus on at this time because the focus of this book is about our children, so be careful tying up your shoes and let's have a look at them.

Without getting too metaphysical, we need to look at and understand why children are born into the families they find themselves in. The two kinds of Karma are:
- **Personal Karma** that is related to why this particular person has chosen to be born into this family at this time.
- **Family Karma** that is related to the overall spiritual development and history of the entire family, actually families because, hopefully the parents are not genetically related.

If you are interested in knowing more about "soul families" Gary Zukav wrote an excellent book called **Seat of The Soul**.

Personal Karma.

Every person, whether they accept it or not is born to mature as an individual on many levels. These levels include physical, mental, emotional and spiritual and maybe some others.

Over the phases of our lives, we will instinctively focus on one of the levels more than the others as dictated by the very nature of our own inner drives, until it is either satisfied or one of the other levels requires moving into the spotlight.

At the time of birth, when the soul has entered the body for this journey, there is a soft spot or opening at the top of the head. This is caused by the two parts of the skull being separated in order to allow the baby's head to fit through the birthing canal. In time, this soft spot will be closed through the maturation of the bone structure of the skull.

During the time the soft spot exists, the individual is downloading important information from the Universe that will help them to be able to express the life they have now embarked up. This information is stored in the mind but managed by the Pituitary Gland, the Master Gland for our entire being.

During this downloading process, this individual will also learn many lessons from the environment they are living in that will also assist in forming their understanding of how to operate during this lifetime.

This information is gained by observing and participating in the life they are playing in with their family and other people who visit in their life. This information is stored in the subconscious mind and is managed by the ego then reported to the pituitary.

Good or bad, the guidelines are now being created and stored that will define how this individual sees and reacts to the world around them. This process generally continues until the child is around seven years of age.

With the combination of downloaded information from the Universe and that from their local environment, this person now sets out to discover their world and why they are here, while looking through the filters they now carry.

Through the information that has been supplied to them, this person has also attained the foundation of their own karma, the obstacle course that will underlie their "raison d'etre" or reason to be in this life.

Family Karma

We all come from a long line of ancestors who have done lifetimes of learning and activities over the thousands of years we humans have existed. It does not matter what these lessons or activities were, we carry the essence of this learning through our genes and our Family Karma.

When we look back at our family history we can see trends regarding our various levels of expression including our looks, our intelligence, how we handle certain situations, even careers.

If you have had a chance to explore your family genealogy, you will find some really interesting things about yourself, especially aspects that are similar to any of your ancestors.

There is a really interesting debate going on currently amongst scientists and psychologists regarding nature versus nurture. Personally, I do not see it as a debate but as two forms of acquiring information and the tools we need to do this life in order to attempt to fulfill our personal life purpose.

The nature aspect related to information acquired through our genes and thus being family karma while nurture is information acquired while learning the ropes of staying alive in the present.

If I ever doubted the importance of the nature aspect of acquiring information, it sure got proven to me recently.

I grew up in a family of four children plus two from a second marriage. It was easy to tell that all six of us were related, although the two youngers had distinct differences. Recently, through these amazing DNA search programs that are now available, I have a new sister!

She is 5 years older than me, but about the same age as my oldest brother. (My daddy was naughty). The day we met changed our worlds. As I walked into the café to meet her, a massive shift occurred as the world stared at a new set of twins!

Trish and I are so similar in personalities, life experiences, and motivations for living and spiritual beliefs. We look and act more like siblings than my other siblings do to me!

I have since introduced her to some of our cousins. Trish now has a twin cousin as well. They even both have the same kinky hair! Every morning Trish looks in the mirror and says good morning to our cousin Colleen!

It is interesting learning about Family Karma as this new relationship unfolds. Our father provided a great deal of learning opportunities for all of his children through his inability to communicate in an effective and positive manner. His ongoing choices to create learning through physical, mental and sexual violence left the four of us original siblings with a lot of fodder to work through.

What is most amazing is that although Trish was raised by a step father who truly loved her and treated her reasonably well, she chose to marry a man who supported her need to endure the same lessons as our father provided for the rest of us, which she missed through growing up elsewhere.

Family Karma!

Understanding our own Karma is essential to creating wellness and evolution in our own lives. It is by understanding the common and prevalent themes that occur or have occurred in our lives and of our predecessors that we become aware of what we need to learn through these situations and bring forward into our lives in a positive manner.

Rather than looking at these situations from a victim perspective (if the lesson is considered bad) we can move away from the emotion and peel back the trauma to unveil an opportunity to grow as a human spirit, by turning it into a positive.

No matter the situation, whether yours or any ancestors, no matter how bad, can be reframed into a positive, by changing the perspective and by understanding what was going on at the time.

One key point to remember in this process is that you are looking at an event from another time through your today eyes. You cannot possibly judge the person for what they did, you can only try to understand and draw a positive from what you can glean. Be sure to keep yourself out of any emotional traps. If you find someone from your past appears to have committed something not acceptable to you, you are not obligated to take on responsibility or guilt for it. Just make sure you choose a better way to express and satisfy the need this person couldn't, if it is deemed part of your path. Only you know for sure.

When we look at the aspect of nurture, it tells us about the methods we have incorporated into our life expression in order to survive and hopefully thrive in this life. As we interact with our environment, we develop rules about survival.

The more emotionally dramatic the childhood learning opportunities, the more nurture has to develop rules in order to cope and survive. This is the basis for personal Karma, at least on the mundane level.

The experience of developing personal karma is different for each child in a family as well, since there are external factors that make each person's experiences different. Pecking order is often one of the most important of these, along with gender as well as what was going on with Mom and Dad during their particular formative time.

If you are interested in learning more about the nurture side, I have written a book called **"Embracing The Blend: What Mom and Dad Didn't Know They Were Teaching You"**.

This book explains two really important aspects for getting through this life alive:
- Understanding and owning your true personal safety
- Understanding and working with your own belief systems

The most important piece of information I can give you regarding Karma is that it is just a starting point and a guide to your own personal evolution for this life time. Karma is not concrete. It is not written in stone! It is written in every moment in your life!

We each have the ability to work with and through our Karma in our own individual way. We are never obligated to suffer needlessly. That is not how Karma works; however, as we live our lives we will make lots of mistakes.

How we choose to deal with these mistakes tells us how we create our Karma.

It is also imperative to understand as we explore our family karma, that we only look at it as an indicator of trends. No person is obligated to follow the family program, however, being aware of such creates the condition where you are aware of the trend, so hopefully, you can do what is necessary to take a different route if it is something you do not want to experience.

A prime example of this situation is diseases. Dr. Bruce Lipton author of The Power of Beliefs is a leading researcher into DNA. His findings state that, just because your family has a propensity for a particular disease, you are not obligated to accept the suffering yourself. Knowing about your family health situations will provide you with tools to ensure optimal health.

Understanding the relationship of beliefs to diseases is a great way to prevent diseases that appear to be common in the family. Louise Hay is a world class leader in this particular field. Her book **You Can Heal Your Life** is essential reading.

Another consideration, especially in regard to health issues but not exclusively, is the location where you or your ancestors spent their lives. Many geographical locations are cesspools for certain diseases, however, your ancestors may not have understood the relationship, so did not know better to leave... I hope you do!

As an example, one is more likely to suffer from the effects of malaria by living in the tropics than by living in the Arctic.

Every person, no matter who they are or what happened to them in their life has free dominion to determine how their life will evolve. It is by understanding the various levels of Karma, along with understanding of the choices they personally make or have made that form the basis of their personal expression, that Karma can be reshaped.

It is the choice of being a victim or a victor in life. Although in truth, the only true position is in being your authentic self!

Through making healthy choices based in awareness, one can move away from a destructive life style pattern into something safer and more meaningful that supports healthier growth opportunities for themselves and the people they influence.

No one is ever obligated to fulfill any thought or impulse they have. We all have free choice and a wonderful conscience to guide us!

Not only do the choices we each make affect the outcome of our own lives, but they also support the energy of change for others.

I am not a Bible person; however, there is much food for thought in this book. Exodus 34:7, explains the "Generational Curse". It says that it takes three generations to eliminate the "Sins of The Fathers" (or mothers).

By choosing to recognize choices made by others, and then consciously making different choices, we give traction to the change process.

This was a decision I made when I became a dad many years ago. My grandchildren are safe because the change I chose to implement so many years ago is working.

I cannot suggest strongly enough, the importance of recognizing the events that shaped your childhood as being learning events rather than reasons to empower victim energy.

If you look at them as lessons, you can then make choices that will foster healthier children for you and your spouse.

Remember, all people are born good. Bad is learned!

210

It is through relationships and belonging to community that we realize our greatest lessons.

Chapter 5

Adult Relationships

I want to separate adult relationships from overall relationships. The focus here is the creation and operation of intimate relationships. Relationships with children, since that is the focus of this book will be discussed separately.

In keeping with the discussion in chapter 1, let's continue asking questions and see if we can get to some reasonable and workable answers.

So, let's start off by asking:

Why do we have relationships? Or more accurately, why do we want to have relationships? How do they relate to the original question "Who are you?"

Wouldn't it be easier if we did not bother interacting with other people and just go off and do our own stuff by ourselves?

As human beings, we have had other people in our lives right from the moment we were born (Actually since we were conceived!). We have had people in our lives right through our childhood and right into our lives today. We have learned to incorporate relationships as a habitual part of how we know life.

We have learned through the process of living our life that having other humans around makes life more tolerable and enjoyable (not there is anything wrong with being alone).

There is a much larger reason for interacting and sharing with other humans as well. It is how we learn and how we grow. Without sharing with others in our lives, we become excessively self-absorbed and therefore limited in our ability to expand our capacity to embrace the larger possibilities of life.

Almost everything we know; we learned through the process of nurturing; learning from our environment and other people. It is also the sharing process that drives people to create and to make life better.

Without having other people to share with, would make the creative process almost pointless, wouldn't it!

On a one to one level or intimate level we create and maintain relationships for more selfish reasons. We want to have our wants, needs and desires met at a much deeper level. Many of these aspects can only be satisfied by interacting with one other person (at least at a time).

An aspect of being alive is that we are a living bundle of energy.

Everything that exists is composed of various frequencies of energy. As human beings, we are composed of many levels of energy that combine together to manifest as life and in our case, conscious life.

As mentioned before, my earlier section about Chakras explains our energetic relationships, so I will not go into too much detail here about the energy side of life, but I do want to share some information about the energy of relationships.

We are very fluid energetically. We absorb energy and we transmit energy constantly throughout our lives.

Part of this process is how we communicate. Speaking and hearing are based on receiving and transmitting energy that our mind can process into thoughts. We can then translate these thoughts into action, if we choose.

We also receive and transmit energy through our other senses including touch, taste and smell. What is often missed in the understanding of this concept though, is that we process energy both physically and non-physically.

In the physical world, we like to communicate using our five senses. However, there is more communication that occurs on the non-physical side that provides much more information than we process physically.

Without the non-physical attributes, life would be very robotic.

Like everything else that exists, we are part of the universe as a whole. Everything we do feeds the universal flow. We draw from the universe, and we give to it by the very nature of our design.

Somewhere along the line we humans, seem to have forgotten that we are directly fed by Universal Source. In its place we have opted to believe that we can only get the energy we need from other people, or maybe our pets.

We have come to rely on using our five senses in interacting with others to attempt to satisfy refueling our energy.

So what does this do to our relationships?

Until we learn to understand and operate our relationships from a more holistic perspective where we include accessing energy from Source, relationships become a battle ground for controlling the energy that flows between two individuals. The more intimate the relationship, the more energies exchanged and the more tug-of-warring that goes on.

How many times have you experienced the ecstasy of a new relationship where there is absolute freedom for all of energy flowing?

So what happens after the honeymoon stage is over?

Right! The fight is on! Whoever can dominate gets the energy and the other suffers until finally the relationship dies.

It does not have to be that way though. Relationships do not have to be a no win struggle!

All we have to do is realize and accept that the energy we crave is ours already. We just have to consciously reconnect with our Source, the Universal Flow of which everything exists.

By reconnecting with Source, we access and absorb the energy we need on our own. This allows us to develop and maintain relationships with others without having to fill a desperate need for an energy fix.

There is no need for a struggle. The relationship then can get on with a more functional focus that is far more satisfying.

So how does one reconnect themselves with Universal Source?

The exercise that is included at the introduction of Chapter 2 is a good place to start. If you do the exercise regularly, you will start to relax more into your body, therefore allowing yourself to feel your true self beyond you external senses.

The next step while doing this exercise is to expand the feeling of being in your body outward beyond the confines of your body.

At first, you can explore the range of your own aura or energy field which normally vibrates out to about 4 feet beyond your physical body.

Once you can feel your aura to some degree, invite another person to join you as you do the exercise. Once you are at the point where you both can feel your own energy field, let your consciousness expand further to see if you can feel the interaction between both of your fields. It will feel sort of like a magnetic pull.

Enjoy this feeling for as long as you wish. It is important to realize that there is no competition in this interaction. You both get to enjoy the feeling equally. This is how relationships are meant to be.

Another fun exercise to try with this is for one person to imagine their aura being really strong and radiant, then to have the other person place their hands in their energy field to try to feel the energy. Eventually, you may even be able to determine which Chakras you are most connected with and which you are not. (These are determiners to what kind of relationship you have currently.)

A final exercise in this matter, is by having both focusing on their energy the holding the palms of their hands toward each other about 4 inches apart will usually let them feel the energy being projected as well.

When we learn to work in relationships in the healthiest way, we will know that our energetic requirements are supplied adequately just because we are designed that way, so, therefore, we can give and receive energy freely with others without fear of running out.

Learning and applying this allows and supports free communication, and keeps us out of the war zone.

When we are comfortable with feeling our own energy field and feeling energetic interactions with others, we can teach our children to do the same thing.

Once we learn to be comfortable with accessing and maintaining our own energy levels through source, it will be more comfortable to let down our guard. After all, isn't our personal energy supply what we are guarding when we pull into ourselves in fear?

Once we are comfortable with this shift, the next step is to learn to observe or witness ourselves. (We actually are quite entertaining!), By observing how we do our life, we become more aware of our strengths and our challenges. Now that we are aware, we can start doing something about them without feeling like our safety is threatened. After all what you are observing are just results of your belief systems.

When we live in our lives in a way that supports our own innate ability to witness ourselves and how we do our lives, we are ready to truly grow in ourselves and make our own life and the world a better place.

218

Passing this ability and perspective on to our children is the reason we are chatting! After all, the better you function in your life, the better your children will function!

When we finally learn to recognize our beliefs as separate from our identity, we can begin to know ourselves in truth.

Chapter 6

Recognizing Our Own Belief Systems

Once we are comfortable with feeling what it is like to actually be in our own bodies we now have a good opportunity to work with ourselves and reframe beliefs that are not working for us.

At this point, I choose to reiterate that I have no desire to tell you what is right or wrong when it comes to beliefs. My only desire, is to provide you with information and some tools that will help you to recognize your own belief systems which will allow you to decide whether they are keepers or not.

I also extend an invitation to you at this point to find yourself some support people to help you move through your stuff. Dealing with belief systems is not something you want to do on your own if you are not experienced in it.

It is not that you are likely to hurt yourself; it is just that you will find it more difficult and more tedious doing it by yourself. At some point, it will likely feel like a big struggle and the tendency to give up will strike, so find yourself a counselor or a support group to help you keep yourself on track!

I have mentioned before my book, **Embracing The Blend**. It has plenty of useful information and tools that will help you understand belief systems and true personal safety.

A note about true personal safety before we move on.

The exercises we have been practicing in this book help you to take yourself to true safety, for the only place you can access true safety is inside yourself, in the manner described. This exercise is not a form of withdrawal or coping. This exercise teaches you how to reconnect with the true safety that is an innate part of your being.

In order to truly be safe, you must believe you are safe because what you believe in your mind determines how safe you feel.

You can do these exercises till the cows come home, but if you do not believe you are safe, you are not.

Using the mantra:

I am safe and protected,

Doing the exercises will help you move into true safety as it helps you focus on being safe. Keep repeating it in groups of threes as often as you need in order to get your mind to believe it and accept it. Be careful not to allow yourself to become obsessive about it, though, as you may be coming from fear rather than encouraging personal strength.

For the purposes of this chapter, the tool we will use for moving past dysfunctional beliefs is similar to the Sun Visualization we have been using. Other exercises you will find useful are available on **my website.**

www.powerfulyoupowerfulme.com

In order to be able to reduce the effect of beliefs and/or undesirable thoughts, you can use the Sun Visualization with an added component. However, before we add this in, we need to understand how thoughts keep you distracted.

First of all, it is essential to understand that you are not your thoughts or emotions.

Remember, we chatted about this in Chapter 1 when we were discussing "Who Are You?"

Thoughts and emotions are what we call temporal. They belong to the outside world and are not part of you. They are not even friends. They are just things. In that, we have the choice about what we do with the thoughts and emotions that play around in our head.

I want to be clear at this point that I am not discounting the importance of thoughts or emotions. They have their place... and they need to stay there. It is not their job to run your life.

So, let's go to the exercise.

Get yourself settled in and take yourself into your quiet place. Once you feel comfortably relaxed and in your body, let yourself feel what is going on inside of you.

Look at the thoughts and feelings you have going on without interacting with them.

The next step is to visualize your sun in the sky again with its rays beaming down on you. Imagine letting those rays melt the thoughts and emotion in your mind until they fade away. It is just like an ice cream cone melting in the summer sun.

As you do this process, continually take comfortable deep breaths, hold it for a bit, and as you slowly exhale, let the thoughts and emotions lose their power and fade away.

Once your mind is quiet and you have relaxed, focus again on your sun and let it fill you up with warm peaceful recharging energy.

Allow the feeling to stay with you as you open your eyes and carry on with your day.

Any time you are feeling caught up in your emotions or thoughts and choose to shift away, this is a great tool to make it happen. The shift can be almost instantaneous if you let it.

Remember, you cannot focus on two things at once, so if you are focusing on your breathing or the feeling of the warm sun on your body, you cannot focus on the thoughts.

Now let's look at belief systems.

The easiest way to recognize belief systems is to listen to your conversations. Any statements that start with "I" are likely belief systems. This is the time to put on your analyst hat and start paying attention to what you are saying.

Remember, you are the only person who gets to listen to your own rhetoric 24/7!

If you find that you are telling yourself the same statement over and over, it might be time to start looking at that statement to determine if it is a good statement for you to be telling yourself.

You might try keeping a journal logging all the statements you are making to yourself. Pay attention as well to what verb follows "I". I believe. I am. I feel.

Of all the phrases in this situation, "I am" requires the most caution for you because it means you are identifying with this statement as part of who you are.

Try to start at the beginning of this journey to replace "I am" with something like "I feel". At least then you are just expressing a feeling instead of identifying with the statement.

If you have decided to join a support group or to work with a counselor, having a list of your common statements will help direct your reframing process. In the meantime, please try to make sure that any statements are supportive and positive.

The goal here is not to rid yourself of beliefs because that would be impossible. The goal is to create a healthy belief system that promotes good health on any level and a good living environment, not just for you but for everyone who is part of your life.

This process is a lifelong practice, so be patient with yourself. Trying to push yourself too hard will only manifest in failure!

One step at a time makes winners!
And remember to breathe!

Your children are an extension of you and your energies and your karma.

Chapter 7

You and Your Children

Why is it so important to understand our relationships and belief systems?

Aren't kids separate individuals from us?

These questions are the key to this whole discussion!

The comingling of the energies of the two individuals who created this little person did more than just create a body and a new person. With this creation comes a union of the energies that each involved person carries with them.

The child in this situation becomes a joining of the karma of both individuals who participated in the creation. This means that not only did they get your fabulous looks and intelligence; they also get their life purpose through the intermixing of your life purposes. **The Celestine Prophecy** is a great book about this subject by James Redfield.

Every person has a life purpose.

It is only by exploring one's own inner drives that allow a person to gain an inkling of what their purpose is. Studying your family genealogy will also help because, if you can get enough information about your ancestors, it will provide clues through their activities about what your purpose is.

Another way that helps determine what your life is likely about is to watch your siblings.

Each of your siblings represents an aspect of your family karma. Watch how they deal with situations in comparison to your own method so you can get a better understanding what you are up to. Learn through their choices and experiences and save yourself the challenge of figuring it out on your own. Again it is about observing your world around you in order to understand who you are and why you are here.

As you observe others, let yourself check how you feel during this period and monitor the thoughts you have. They are key clues to finding your life purpose.

Your life purpose may not be a career move or any other outward expression. It might just be a need to recognize many shifts over your life that need to be made in order to maximize your self-expression and your feelings of self-empowerment.

Why do I care about all this?

The very fact that you are this far in reading this book should tell you something about the answer to this question! This is not a book you would read just before going to bed, so you are definitely in questioning mode.

Being that you are this far into this book, it should be safe to assume that you are a person who is questioning your life and looking for answers about why you are here.

For me, this has been a lifelong quest. Part of my karma is to write and publish these books to help you and others to understand and maximize your experience on this planet. Ask questions... and let the answers arrive!

Do you have any idea what your life purpose is?

Deep down inside you know that your highest purpose is to gain maximum personal and spiritual growth, not only for yourself and your partner but for your children as well... and every other person you interact with.

Now all you have to do is figure out what that path is.

We all love our children very deeply. The information in this book will assist you in being the great parent you desire to be. Through having a good idea of what your life is about, as well as your partner's, you can help your children to find and express their purpose.

The best way to help your children through this process is the answer to the question that caused you to pick up this book to start with.

What are The Three Things Healthy Children Need?

It is finally time to have a look at these three aspects!

Chapter 8

The First Need

Let's have a good look at each of these needs separately, so we can focus on each one individually.

We have already been discussing the first need since the beginning of our discussion in this book.

Healthy Children Need Parents Who Are Aware of Themselves and Growing as People.

Children model themselves after their parents and key caregivers. Children are like insatiable sponges when it comes to learning. Children will learn regardless of the situation they are born into.

The concern for parents should be about what kind of situation the child is being born into, because this will be a deciding factor in what they learn... and how they will deal with life.

A cautionary statement!!!

There is no such thing as a perfect person, parent or situation. The purpose of this book is only to inspire and support you, the reader, to be the best person you can be. We will leave the perfect person, parent and situation to the folks who live in that illusion.

The best we can do is the best we can do... at the time. We could have all done better when we look back; however, life isn't about looking back. Life is about being present now, as we travel through our lives.

As we live our lives, we become aware of situations where we really excel. We also become aware of situations where we really suck... and everything in between. A person who chooses to be aware and proactive in building a good life accepts each awareness as a witness and makes the necessary adjustments as they can and choose.

Besides, who is in charge of determining what is acceptable and what is not?

It is up to each individual to make their own decisions. In making these decisions though, as a parent and as a partner in an intimate relationship, it is important to include your spouse in the discussion (once you have clarity about your situation).

The next step is to determine what effect the choice to be made has on each individual impacted, especially the children. No time for egos here!

Let's have an example.

Mom used to be a smoker. She remembers how she used to enjoy puffing on her cigarettes. Mom decides that she wants to start smoking again, so she goes to the store to buy a pack. On the way, she recalls the agreement she has with her family that any big decisions are to be discussed before going ahead, so she decides to wait on the purchase.

When her family is home in the evening, she broaches the subject with her family.

Immediately tension fills the air. Dad says he does not like the second hand smoke, and he does not like kissing an ashtray. The kids echo his sentiments. Besides mom would have to smoke outside, so she would not be as available to interact with the kids during that time, and they don't like how she would smell when she came back in.

Mom takes all this in, and takes some time to digest what they have told her. She then realizes that the reason she liked to smoke was because it made her feel like she was part of the gang who used to hang out together to smoke.

Her real desire was to be acceptable and accepted.

Mom also realized the health risks involved in taking up smoking again, not only for herself but also her family, so it did not take her long to realize the choice she would make.

She realized that she needed to work on her resistance to feeling accepted, especially important since she now realized she did not need to smoke in order to be accepted in her most important gang... her family.

What kind of decision does dad need to make in his life? Well dad wants to buy a boat and go fishing, so he calls the family together .

The kids loved the idea, except that dad wasn't thinking about taking them with him all the time. Mom is nervous about the idea because it is a big expense. However, everyone puts their emotions aside and agrees to discuss the matter.

The final agreement that wins everyone's support, including dad's, is that the family will join the local hunting and fishing club, so they can each enjoy participating in nature sports with others. Dad gets to go fishing with his new buddies sometimes because he does need "guy time" while mom enjoys making new friends at the club while not spending thousands of dollars unnecessarily... and the kids learn to enjoy some great outdoor sports. Everybody wins!

When the parents are aware of their wishes and are inclusive of their family in the decision making process, the opportunity for each member to grow increases.. not to mention the bonding that occurs!

And this opens up the conversation to the second need!

238

239

Healthy kids need to not only feel safe, but they also need to have a safe environment in order to flourish.

Chapter 9

The Second Need

In my first book, **Embracing The Blend**, I spent a great deal of time discussing this very subject.

Safety

So what is a safe environment?

In my childhood, staying out of the way was safe. My father had a real tendency to use his hands as his primary form of communication. I spent the bulk of my childhood in my bedroom. My older brother, on the other hand, spent much of his youth in jail for exactly the same reason.

So, what is safety?

I call it true safety in order to distinguish it from other methods of so-called being safe.

True safety is innate. You are born with it. The slogan of my Embracing The Blend book is:

We are born into safety… Then trained out of it… Now it is time to return!

True safety is the process of creating and maintaining an ongoing environment where anyone who participates in that space can relax and take comfort in being themselves without having to be constantly aware of any issues where they might need to protect themselves or others.

This environment not only allows the participants to feel safe but to be able to (within reasonable guidelines) experiment with life in order to grow as a person.

Pretty well anything outside of this definition would be called "protective safety" or "coping".

As human beings, we are very capable of creating safe environments for ourselves and for others without having to resort to protective practices or coping strategies like medications or hiding in the bedroom.

Healthy children come equipped with the ability to fit in. What they do not have is the ability at younger ages to determine whether their "fitting in" tactics are truly safe or acceptable. It is up to the parents to guide and train them in these matters.

What do children want from their family?

I feel that I need to say at this time that "love" is not the answer. We all want love; however, the truth is that love is an innate part of who we are. We always have love; it is just a matter of how the love is expressed that causes concern.

Whatever we experience as children that gives us the attention we desire is what we know as love… until we learn differently.

A wonderful book on this very subject is **I'm Okay, You're Okay**. It discusses a psychological process called Transactional Analysis. The key point in this book is that children will get the attention they desire. The question is will they get it through positive attention or through discounted attention by acting out.

According to the author, Thomas Anthony Harris, children will derive that attention from acting out even though it takes many times as much effort as positive attention, just because that is what they perceive is necessary to get that much needed attention in their immediate circumstances.

The answer? Pay positive attention to your kids! Help them feel included.

Children need positive, healthy boundaries: Consistent boundaries that expand as they mature through the experience of living their life and making choices.

Why do we put small children in playpens?

To give them boundaries!

A playpen is a physical boundary designed to help that child be safe. The child (and the parent) can be more relaxed when the child is in the playpen because they can see the physical boundaries that they can play in. The child can feel that the parent is more relaxed so they can focus on exploring their own little world without concern for safety.

As the child ages, they outgrow the playpen, but they do not outgrow the need for boundaries.

Would you let your five year old child drive your car? Of course not. This is a boundary!

Would you let your five year old child have free rein in your laptop? Of course not!

However, you would let this child explore his home environment (under your watchful eye) and let him figure out what his world is all about. As the child learns to crawl, and then to walk, the boundaries are expanded to allow for more growth. This process should be an ever expanding process, until such a time as this person is a fully mature adult.

Children need to have consciously decided boundaries determined by their parents that support the child's ability to be as safe as possible while exploring their world at the current level they are at.

There may be many people who do not agree with me; but I am going to state it anyway. I believe that children are not equal to their parents when it comes to having the right to make decisions about their lives, or how they choose to express themselves.

I personally believe that rights and privileges are earned. Children do have the right to be treated lovingly, respectfully and to explore their world in an acceptable manner to the parents.

In the process of maturing, children need and want to expand their boundaries and will push to find those boundaries.

Parents need to understand and manage what the parameters of those boundaries are at any given time. They need to be consistent, and they need to be willing to interact maturely with the child to discuss reasons for the boundaries as the child matures.

Although I certainly support children's rights, children are only as mature as their internal development supports. In that, a person who is not fully mature does not have the capacity or faculties to make decisions at the same level as a mature person.

Children should be supported constantly to make decisions; however, their decision needs to be rubber stamped by the parents as a means of protecting the child from unnecessary harm and undesirable learning experiences.

When children are raised to understand and accept the pecking order, they will be happier themselves and the home environment will benefit. NO discounting!

I think if we were to go look at the statistics, wherever they are, regarding children who get into trouble, we will definitely find a parallel between the appropriate setting and maintaining of healthy boundaries and the acting out of the involved children.

Children need to be treated like people. As adults, we need to realize and accept that children do not have the understanding, experience or processing skills that we have. We, therefore, need to communicate with them in a manner that is at their level.

This does not mean talking to them in baby talk. It does mean physically getting yourself down to their level when you talk to them, especially with very young children.

I would presume that you might have noticed that most adults are considerably bigger than children. When a much bigger adult goes off the deep end and starts ranting or barking orders, the child becomes afraid and will do whatever it can to protect itself.

Can you imagine what it looks like and feels to a small person when the much larger adult who towers over them (and is supposedly their protector) acts out in a way that is terrifying to them? Of course, they are going to act out! They feel afraid!

When it becomes a regular occurrence, it becomes a part of their belief system. They will automatically react to anything even similar to this learned experience. They feel unsafe!

Another point I wish to make, as well, is about how children communicate.

Young children who are not at the stage of speaking yet, still express themselves. It just is not in the form we are used to communicating in. It is our job to communicate with them in a way they understand. They just want to be heard!

Later in this section I have included some techniques one can use for communicating with small children in a manner that overrides the need for them to speak verbally.

I recall one time walking down the street in a city that was known for its hills. A mom was walking near me with her son who was about 4 years of age, as well as with a toddler who was safely nestled in the stroller. The little boy was a typical little guy who wanted to run about everywhere.

As they were heading down the hilly sidewalk, he kept bolting ahead. Of course, mom was worried about his safety but could not manage him adequately because of the stroller.

She kept yelling at him "Stop" "Stop" "Stop"... but of course he did not.

Everything turned out okay and she finally got him settled down but as I watched this episode I wondered if the little boy even knew what the word "stop" means?

The mom was making a presumption that could have been very costly!

One of my favorite situations happened in front of me involving my friend's son-in-law and his daughter.

The son-in-law is a big guy, about 6 ft 3. His daughter was about 2 ½ years old at the time. We were in a big store shopping when all of a sudden the daughter started screaming and acting out.

Very quickly, the dad got himself right down to the daughter's level, reached his hand gently out for her to grab without touching her, then quietly invited her to come to him.

He just stayed in that position until she finally settled down and reached into him. Once she was feeling safe but still screaming, he asked her what it was she wanted. She kept pointing and screaming.

Again, quietly, he spoke to her and told her that he did not understand her screaming and that if she wanted him to understand she would have to "use her words". He then continued to sit there until she stopped screaming. She then took a deep breath and, in her words, told him her concerns.

Dad then remedied the situation and we all carried on. Eventually, the daughter learned that screaming was not a functional form of communication and chose to use her words instead.

The lesson inside these examples is that children need to understand and know they are safe. Although safety is a natural function of our subconscious mind, it still requires a great deal of persistence in training the children what it really means to be truly safe.

Children need to have and to know consistent boundaries that are applied lovingly, continuously and appropriately for their level of maturity.

For older children, this still holds true, however, a big concern to me in our society today is that older children are often taught to believe that they have the same rights to act and express themselves as the adults do.

I again reiterate that children, no matter their age, only have the rights and privileges they have earned. This sense of entitlement that is the rage in our society today is having catastrophic outcomes and needs to be reined in.

If we continue with this lack of boundaries, our society will continue to degrade, and our economy and society will falter as children are unable and unwilling to participate in a mature, helpful manner that contributes to the wonderful life created for them.

As it is, we are raising a section of society that unjustly feels privileged and not obligated to have considerations for the rules of society and the rights of others.

The only way to prevent this from becoming engrained is to start training children from the earliest years to respect themselves and any others.

Children who are raised in a safe environment do not grow up to be gang members, or dangerous drivers, homeless or parasites on society.

Children raised in safe environments grow up to be healthy, prosperous, engaged individuals who truly embrace and enjoy life and help to foster such feelings in others.

Before we leave the topic of safety and the development of healthy boundaries, I feel that it is important to bridge a conversation regarding a very popular topic of today.

I recently came across two wonderful examples of how appropriate boundaries and fostering have helped children to become the amazing people they are so capable and desirous of being.

A friend of mine has a 3 year old grandson... who already is a capable... downhill skier!!!

I was recently watching a live hockey game being played by some young children roughly between the ages of 5 and 10. They were girls playing!!!

In both of these situations, how well would these children be doing if they did not have appropriate parenting and a solid understanding of the importance of rules?

This next topic is about parenting itself.

How many people does it take to raise a child in a healthy manner?

We live in a very complicated society where every person seems to believe they have the right to do what they want and do it how they want and that is okay.

This is ego based thinking. Unfortunately, most of this kind of thinking is just rebellious and does not work for anyone involved.

It takes a man and a woman to create a child. Children are born with the essence of male and female inside them in their creation. Children need to have the influences of both males and females in their lives in order to grow and mature into healthy individuals.

I want to be clear that my intention is not to be condescending toward single parenting or homosexual parenting. My purpose is to point out that because children have both a male and female aspect inside themselves, they need to have both a positive male and a positive female influence over the long term of their maturing process in order to fully know and be their true and complete selves.

A man or a woman, no matter their sexual orientation, cannot provide the essence of the other gender no matter how they try. It just is not in them. Only a woman can provide female essence and only a man can provide the male essence.

Even though, in the grand scheme of our design, we do carry the programming and capacities of both the sexes, our minds are principally oriented by the gender of our body. Even in homosexuals, men and women think and operate differently.

If a child is raised in a single parent environment, for the child to be healthiest, the child needs to have a person of the other gender (and preferably someone in for the long-haul) to balance their needs. The two people do not need to live together but they do need to work together to give this child the best shot at life.

In homosexual relationships, the same needs to be applied as in a single parent relationship.

If we truly wish for our children to have the best chance in succeeding in all levels of life, we need to be open and willing to allow other people to be involved in their upbringing.

Even in heterosexual partnerships with children, the child gains a wider perspective in life if there are more caregivers involved in the raising of that child. Aunts, uncles, older siblings, grandparents and good friends can provide essential support for a child while giving Mom and Dad a well-deserved break. After all, raising children is more than a full time job!

In providing a safe environment for a child, it is essential that the parents create a safe, supportive and comfortable environment for themselves too!

A truly safe environment for children needs to include other people, so they can learn to feel safe to explore the world outside of the environment created by Mom and Dad.

After all, the little bird must fly from the nest one day! Simulating the outside world in a managed and effective way provides the basic structure for the child to manage its role in the outside world.

251

People are like plants. They need the right place, the right conditions and lots of love to grow and prosper.

Chapter 10

The Third Need

We are finally getting down to the nitty gritty of providing for the needs of healthy children!

When adults know themselves and are committed to advancing themselves as human beings and when these people choose to create and raise children in a truly safe environment, the most important aspect of caring for the needs of the children can be made manifest.

The third need for healthy children is:

An environment that provides and encourages their own personal growth through experiences in life.

Whether we choose to believe it or not, we are born into this life to grow in our own individual manner. By design, we are committed to become the most we are capable of becoming as a human being or human spirit. However, life has a way of getting in the way.

By default, all people, no matter their age or circumstance will always do what they need to do in order to feel safe. When children are not provided with a truly safe and respectful environment, they learn to cope. Their need to "feel" safe is either their first priority or their only priority. The fear of not feeling safe is so powerful that it can override all other occurrences. Their coping becomes their mechanism for safety.

It is up to us as parents to be conscious of our own methods of getting through life and ensuring that our offspring develop and express outcomes that serve them in the best possible way.

When children are born, their mind is basically an empty slate. It is up to their parents to develop and implement an ongoing plan to ensure that the children in their charge are provided with the very best opportunities to become the amazing people they already are.

This does not mean having to send them to the best schools and dress them in the best, most fashionable outfits or provide them with every bobble that the big guns say they have to have in order to be truly acceptable to their peers.

It does mean spending plenty of quality time with them, interacting in meaningful ways such as chatting, cooking, teaching them how to do useful things, going for walks in nature, and, most important, helping them to explore their own interests in life.

Every child is born with a special set of interests that are brought forward through their own karma. It is our job as parents and care givers to help each child to work their way through a myriad of adventures while observing, testing and unveiling the story that lies inside this person.

It is our job to help each child to discover and understand who they are. This again falls into the development of boundaries. Boundaries are safe when consistently applied; however, boundaries also need to make sense and should be appropriate to their age.

Children need to understand and accept basic concepts about themselves that help them to define themselves. In this statement, I also reserve the aspect of maintaining a more open set of boundaries that support self-knowledge.

Inside this self –knowledge, there is room to play as part of the exploring.

Now I know I am going to get flack for stating my perspective on this subject, but I do it in respect with a desire for common sense.

Here goes!

There are two aspects to human beings. As I have previously stated, these are the physical and non-physical. The physical aspect is what we can see as well as what we perceive as our methodology for interacting in this world. This includes our physical senses and emotions.

This non-physical aspect I am referring to is the soul.

The soul has no gender. The only purpose of the soul in a living being is to collect information with which it grows and becomes stronger as part of the Cosmic Whole.

The gender of a normal healthy person is determined and validated simply by looking between the infant's legs. Animals of any kind including human beings only come in two genders: male and female.

It is important for children to understand their gender because they will naturally and predominantly express the nature of that gender in their lives. It seems that usually boys like trucks and girls like dolls. However, there is no shame at all in little boys playing with dolls or girls liking to play with trucks after all; being male or female is not an exact science.

As their life progresses, they will gravitate to activities that express their true nature, as long as the parents consciously guide, support and give them supported space along the way.

Providing a safe environment that includes lots of exploratory discussions will help the child to make choices and mold their life according to their inner drives.

As children mature, so must the conversations. When puberty arrives, the discussions and the training need to be ramped up. With the onset of all those hormones that occur during this period, a lot of chaos ensues.

The child in puberty is faced with a lot of unknowns that they need to sort out. Your being there for them with an open, supportive and knowledgeable mind will help them through this time in the best manner possible.

I think one of the biggest mistakes we make in helping our children grow is to rush them into being grown up too fast. This is a social issue. We are inundated with television shows depicting teens acting like adults, when they clearly are not.

With a great deal of love, respect and conversation inside the family setting, these children can get a whole lot better perspective on life from their family life than they can from a television show. The end result will be happier and healthier adults who can then perpetuate the healthy kids program.

The ultimate goal in raising our children is to be mentors for them so they can grow to become all they can be. Creating and maintaining a fluid structure that supports each of the children in their own way helps them to feel safe. When children feel safe, they can more easily focus on exploring their worlds and determining how they want to express their lives.

When children do well with their lives as they progress along, they are easier to live with, do better in school, have better friends and become better grownups.

Inevitably, issues are going to arise from time to time, as life has a way of providing us with unscheduled learning opportunities. Children are going to act in ways that are not acceptable to the parents at times. Welcome to life.

If we remember as we engage in these challenging times, that they are just learning situations and that as we each engage in the situation in a safe, supportive and respectful manner, the situation will be handled so everyone grows, and the situations easily becomes history.

Remember, the only reasons children act out are because they are looking for boundaries or if they find themselves in a situation they do not have enough life experience to handle well.

When they push against a current boundary, it is going to challenge the parents' authority. Handled incorrectly, it magnifies the problem.

Recognize the situation for what it is, handle it correctly through positive interactive engagement and the issue is dealt with. Love them and help them to learn life in a constantly up reaching manner, so they feel loved, challenged and inspired.

The overall growth of a child needs to include recognition and training on all levels of their person. This can be a little tricky if a person is not "religious". Many healthy families understand and work well in providing their children with good training in the physical, mental and emotional realms but tend to fall short in the spiritual realm.

It is not my purpose at this point to direct anyone towards religion. It is my point to point out that religion is only a tool that provides direction toward spirituality.

In respect to all, each person must choose any of the paths that work for them according to their needs and their perception of life. Since this is not a discussion about the pros and cons of religion, I will leave it at that.

Spirituality is a completely separate topic. I feel that it is important to include spirituality in the process of raising children. It is completely up to the parents as to how this will be implemented.

I am going to include my perspective of where and how spirituality can be included as a non-religious activity.

To me, spirituality means connection with all that exists.

Everything that exists is connected to me and I am connected to all else. Therefore when I interact with other people, I choose to come from a place of respect and connection. I choose to care about myself and others as I engage with them.

I am also a part of nature. I am a part of nature as a part of the animal kingdom and choose to engage from this perspective. I embrace all nature and revel in its beauty. I feel responsible for the destruction we are causing on this planet and choose to help to improve our situation.

I feel life, I feel the life force within me. I feel the life force within you. I feel the life force in the world around me.

This is spirituality. If you choose to add any formalized structure to that, so be it.

259

Giving, and consciously supporting, the widest berth to your children to allow them to grow in the best way possible to become the best expression they can manifest is our most important job as parents.

Loving and supporting your kids enough to let them be and become themselves in their most fulfilling way is our ultimate goal!

Chapter 11

Summing up How to Raise amazing children.

Love is the one thing we think we all desire, and yet, it is the one thing we always have.

As human beings, we seem to have been blessed with the ability to hide what we most want in plain sight. After all, love is an innate aspect of who we are, and is the basis of everything that exists.

The challenge I offer to you, after reading this book, is for you to find the real love that always has existed in your life.

This may require contemplating what we mean by love. It may also require your investigating how you perceive and integrate love into your life.

We are never without love.

We are often without understanding.

It is our job as adult human beings and as parents to discover how we interpret love in our life.

It is through becoming detached from our belief systems that we can gain clarity about how we do our lives and how we give and receive love.

We learned the art of loving through our relationships with our parents and other caregivers. It is our responsibility to ensure that the love we give to our children is what we truly want for ourselves.

By actively loving our children, we set the intention of knowing ourselves and making healthy choices. We do the best to provide a safe environment that grows and expands with each child as they learn how to live in their own lives.

We implement actions in our lives and the lives of our children that assist and support them in the process of coming to know themselves, their world and what they can become as healthy, responsible adults.

It is by helping ourselves to love, it is by teaching our children to be loving beings that the world will heal. By getting beyond our "selves", we can integrate in the energy of love and consciously help to expand it throughout our universe.

It is only through love that we can truly exist and flourish. It is only through true safety that we can ever truly know true love.

There is more tools available for raising children than your mind knows. And yet, these new tools are just a different way of using your mind!

Bonus Section

Tools for Effective Parenting

Some of the information in this chapter may seem like a reiteration of information we have already discussed; however, these are important points that lead to the most important point in this chapter... developing non-physical tools for managing your relationships.

In this section, we will discuss various aspects that will assist you in helping your child be the amazing child they were born to be. By being a proactive, committed and consciously involved parent, you will get the best reward of all, a happy child!

Psychologists say that over 80% of all communication occurs non-verbally. Use this to your advantage.

The first step in being the best parent possible is to acknowledge that each of you are a shining example of the gender you are. Therefore, your children will model that aspect of themselves through how they interpret what they extract from you.

Have you ever watched a man and his son walking together? The likelihood is they walk the same gait. Why?

The son learned it from watching his dad, so he copied it.

Being aware of this fact should not be scary! If you feel the pressure just increased on your demand to be a great parent, this is a time to recognize your own self-perspective.

Just be yourself! Choose to be relaxed and good with how you express your life. Just be mindful that your children are watching you.

Here is an example of where a parent could have been more mindful:

A dad and his son were out riding their bikes. The son was riding well just following along behind dad... right through a stop sign!

How is dad going to feel when:
 a) son gets hit by a car doing the same thing
 b) son gets into accidents while driving a car from not following the rules
 c) son gets into trouble at school for disobeying rules.

It all boils down to the same thing!

Dad set the example that rules do not apply to him! Son is only copying him!

On the other side- Dad religiously gets up extra early every morning, so he can do his set of exercises and get outside and run 10 miles before work. As son gets old enough, dad encourages son to finally join him after years of casually mentioning how great it feels.

How is this son going to behave?

He loves his dad and follows his example. The likelihood is that this boy will mature into a healthy individual.

Children do have the ability to choose, and they will choose incorrectly. That is part of the process. They need to learn what is right and what is wrong. They also need to learn what works for them as part of exploring their own personal perspective of the world.

Each child will learn some things from the mom and some from the dad and some they will figure out themselves. Welcome to life!

As a parent, it is our duty to observe the child and guide them gently to choose which is truly best for them. This may mean letting them make many mistakes, but not letting them give up on themselves because it is too hard.

This does not mean forcing them to follow the family traditions! They do not have to take up the career that one of the parents has... unless they show a strong interest and aptitude for it.

When a child shows an unacceptable trait, it is usually one of two things:

a) a cry for attention
b) they are experimenting, trying to do something they do not have a clear concept of.

Your job is to recognize what they are doing and why!

Recognize the emotion attached to the activity. Reading their facial expression and any body language will give you clues. Monitor the situation, discuss it with your spouse and when the appropriate time occurs, guide the child lovingly and patiently to resolve the issue.

Children need boundaries! They crave boundaries and will push to find them. Even in this modern world of allowing children to make their own choices, they want and need their parents to love them enough by showing them boundaries!

You, as parents, need to determine what those boundaries are and to keep them in place, relaxing them only as you see fit, depending on the child's maturity.

If you start right from the birth of the child consciously placing boundaries on the child's actions, the child will become an easier person to interact with. Keeping your child in a playpen to limit their mobility is much better than disciplining the child for getting into mischief.

However, putting enough toys in the playpen to keep them happily busy is a must or they will tell you, in no uncertain terms, they are bored.

By consciously making good decisions regarding boundaries, the child will be more settled and happier thus making your life more pleasant.

Once we have the general atmosphere worked out, the emotional levels will be much easier to manage and live with. This now opens the door to using tools that have not commonly been offered to parents that will assist in keeping things happy, positive, and best for all.

The Non-Physical tools

As was stated earlier, about 80% of all training for the child occurs non-verbally. This leads us to the concept that the true training of a child should largely be focused on non-verbal triggers.

The most important non-verbal key is your own display of emotions. Be real, as life is generally not a perfect expression, but be mindful that ongoing displays of anger, control and other less than preferable actions will be absorbed and reflected in the child.

Everyone wants to feel safe. When a child feels the energy of a less than desirable emotion, whether directed at them or not, their feeling of safety is disrupted.

A safe child is an easy child to live with. When children have an ongoing challenge of feeling safe in what they perceive as an unsafe environment, they are going to be far more difficult to live with.

If you and/or your spouse does not feel safe and commonly expresses emotions that are challenging to the child, it would be best for both of you to get help and access tools that will help you to become more stable expressions.

The exercises posted on my website: www.powerfulyoupowerfulme.com/videos are valuable tools to assist you in managing the activities of your mind. Learning how to release and reframe undesirable beliefs will help you express yourself as a more wholesome and healthier individual and parent.

Other activities such as physical exercise, walks in nature, meditation, playing games with your children and others where a sense of positive energy is expressed will help you and your child feel safer.

If you would like to learn more about your belief systems and how to manage them, please read my book: Embracing The Blend. Our mind works exactly the same way a computer does. This book provides great information about how your personal software works and how you can manage it.

After all, you are born with the ability to manage and make changes in how your mind works. You just need to know you can and then implement the tools to be able to make the changes you desire.

The next non-verbal tool that is essential to managing and nurturing your child is touch.

Human beings love to be touched. The first choice in being touched is always positive touch. The laying of a hand on them gently for no particular reason, messing up their hair just for the fun of it, a big hug are all examples of positive touch.

Positive touch should always be done with no ulterior motives. Children are sensitive to the truth. If an action has a negative intent to it, they will pick it up!

Scruff up your child's hair or give them a hug just because you wish to express that you love them!

The Psychic Side of Human Communication

There is another side to non-verbal communication which goes on whether we choose to recognize it or not, therefore it is best to recognize it and use it as a positive tool.

That tool is your own psychic ability!

We all have a psychic side. It is just another layer of our ability to communicate information between each other. It does not require taking courses to become a psychic. Much of the basic information you need you have already read in the section about Chakras.

You can use these tools when interacting with any person, including yourself. The goal is always to assist them in feeling more positive and safer. The more positive a person is, the easier they are to get along with.

Here are some tools you can work with to deal with specific situations:

Communicating with babies

Learn to understand what babies are saying when they are verbalizing. Whether it is general chatter or crying, they are attempting to communicate with you. If you listen quietly to the communication they are offering, you will learn to understand what they are trying to tell you. This is particularly true of crying. If you take the time to learn the different sounds of their cries, you will soon pick up what their message is. Believe me, the cry from a dirty diaper is quite different from one of pain or from being hungry!

Communicating with children in distress

If a child is in distress, of course, you will know what they want so you can help them. Sometimes, they are just wanting attention, so here is a technique that you can do from a distance, particularly at night.

Visualize yourself standing near the child, take a series of deep breaths while visualizing rubbing their back in a downward stroke. You can imagine them in a cloud of gold light as well if you like. Very quickly, they will pick up the energy and relax. The downward stroke helps to ground them to the earth. Communication is fulfilled without even getting out of bed!

Increasing your intention to connect with another person.

Visualize sending gold light to a person you wish to increase your connection with. (Always with no ulterior motive)

Helping one another to deal with a situation without verbally interacting.

Send the same gold light to a person who is struggling with some issue. It is essential that when you send this gold light that you send it with no other intention than to support them in moving through whatever is causing them to need your support. Potentially manipulative thoughts and gold light do not mix!

Sending your child positive thoughts non-verbally to help them grow.

Send your child positive messages through your mind to theirs without verbalizing. Keep the messages simple and clear. "I love you unconditionally", "I choose to know and accept the real you", "Let yourself be", "Be safe" are all forms of positive messages you can send to your child. These are especially effective while they are sleeping. You can sit near them on their bed and silently project the thoughts to them.

The most important aspect of working with you child, or any other person, is to be sincere and honest in your communication.

Know you own desires. Know your own agenda before you attempt to use any of these tools. Be clear!

A child who is constantly raised in an imperfect but positive environment will be an easier person to know and love. It all starts with you!

Please be intentional parents!

Ponderings

Some of these questions might provoke some emotion when reading and working through them. Please consider them as opportunities to know yourself better. Please get help from a counselor if needed.

Why did you choose to become a parent?

Can you recognize similarities in your style of parenting to what you learned when you were a child?

Are any of the techniques you employ based in fear rather than the love you wish to base your life on?

Do you react to situations with your child unconsciously or out of habit?

Do you consciously provide healthy learning opportunities for your child that are suitable for their age?

Are there ways you react to situations that could be done better so your child can develop a better toolkit for their life?

How many caregivers are actively participating in your child's life?

Do the other caregivers provide positive nurturing for your child?

Do these caregivers have specific roles?

How do you and your partner share parenting?

Do you plan out how you wish to raise your child, or do you live in the moment?

How do you come to agreement regarding the life path choices for your child?

How do you decide appropriate boundaries?

277

In Summary

Throughout this book I have provided information to provoke thought and action. As human beings living in this most wonderous time, I feel we need to prepare ourselves to be in a position to handle what is coming up, and more importantly, to teach our children how to thrive in this new energy.

By learning to build a truly functional relationship between our mind and our body, we will awaken to the tools and concepts we need to more than just survive, but to live our lives to the fullest.

If one lives their life like a mechanic or a carpenter having all the tools needed to function and thrive in daily life, we all stand a better chance of growing the best way possible, no matter what lies ahead.

I truly hope that the information in this book has spurred you into action to take charge of your life, get past the lies that are pervasive in our world today and really become the person you are capable of being so that your inner light shines so brightly that it attracts others to the possibilities of a wonderful new world based in the essence of Love.

After all, we are all in this together. For it is through the creation and maintenance of true community that we will continue to co-exist here on Mother Earth.

If the predictions of many of the futurists are even remotely correct, we must learn how to see the truth in what manifests around us. We must be prepared to make the best possible choices for maintaining our personal integrity.

By making the choice to accept self-realization as a path to the greatest truth, we also build that truth in our children. Only truly enlightened people will survive the onslaught of insults that are pending.

As I stated earlier, this cusp will last about 350 years, so we still have about 300 years to go. We who are alive today will not see the full inception of the Age of Aquarius, at least not in this current body, however, our descendants will.

It is up to us to prewrite the future by accepting, learning and teaching self-realization to our children. By incorporating honest self-realization into our own thinking and processing, it becomes part of our DNA. This DNA will become the fuse to light the torch for your future generations!

Namaste

Monty

2

3

About The Author

Monty Ritchings specializes in helping people understand what drives them. For over thirty years Monty has been a practicing energetic healing facilitator, core belief counselor, medical intuitive and facilitator of programs that assist people in understanding and empowering their own inner self.

As a proud dad and grandpa, Monty treasures watching his family and the families of friends grow and reveal the beauty and true nature of each of the people involved.

As our world changes and evolves, Monty writes and publishes books and booklets in hopes that the words help to raise the consciousness of the human species.

Monty's website is www.powerfulyoupowerfulme.com.

Books by Monty C. Ritchings

Available through your favorite online bookstore!

Embracing The Blend

What Mom and Dad Didn't Know They Were Teaching You

Published 2007 Revised 2009 Revised 2019.

Stamp Out Stress

Living With Stress is a Choice, Not a Fact of Life

Published 2010 Revised 2019

Let's Get Hiking!

A Guide For Serious Walkers and Hikers

Published 2015 Revised 2019

Chakras Demystified

Our True Communication System Revealed!

Published 2019

Healthy Children Only Need Three Things

Published 2020

The Ascenders Return To Grace Series

Book 1 2021   Book 2 2022   Book 3 2024

6

These videos and more are available on the website at and on my YouTube channel "Powerful You Powerful Me"

Conscious Mind Management
Living in Present Time
Quieting The Mind

www.ingramcontent.com/pod-product-compliance
Lightning Source LLC
Chambersburg PA
CBHW080917170426
43201CB00016B/2177